HOW TO BECOME A SCIENTIST

The PhD and Postdoc years

Jonathan Bard

Emeritus professor, University of Edinburgh
Graduate advisor, Balliol College, Oxford

- networks are important for:
  - day to day survival
  - job apps & research collabs
  -
- managing upwards

can we get 2 postdocs in?
do they use 2nd supervisor?

> I thank my wife, Professor Gillian Morriss-Kay, for our many discussions about becoming a scientist and for her pithy comments on the manuscript. I am also grateful to all my colleagues and generations of graduate students who have shown me what does and what does not work.

Things to look up:-
- Resilience as a scientist/researcher
- can we make this look like a prize? Attach prizes to the programme?
- Research here, or research anywhere?
- profiles of each student
- can we give them copies of this book? £3/£6.50
- are they happy with me sharing honestly, y objectives?
- Mary Allen. Nature
- finda phd → handling supervisors.

© 2019 Jonathan Bard. All rights reserved.

CONTENTS

How to Become a Scientist	1
Dedication	3
Copyright	4
Forward	8
Section 1	11
Chapter 1: Starting a career in science	12
Chapter 2: Doing research	18
Chapter 3: Planning your CV	24
Chapter 4: Plagiarism and cheating	30
Section 2	37
Chapter 5: The MSc year	38
Chapter 6: Thinking about a PhD	48
Chapter 7: Choosing a lab and a supervisor for a PhD	55
Section 3	63
Chapter 8: Choosing a PhD research project	64
Chapter 9: The first year of a PhD	68

Chapter 10: Handling supervisors	81
Chapter 11: The second year of a PhD – just research	90
Chapter 12: The final year of a PhD	100
Chapter 13: When things go wrong	111
Chapter 14: Writing your first paper	124
Chapter 15: Writing up a PhD thesis	134
Chapter 16: PhD exams	149
Section 4	159
Chapter 17: The postdoc decision	160
Chapter 18: Applying for a postdoc	168
Chapter 19: Succeeding as a postdoc	172
Chapter 20: Alternative careers	181
Chapter 21: Second postdocs, fellowships and beyond	185
Section 5	196
Chapter 22: Luck	197
Chapter 23: A life in science	204
Section 5	208
Chapter 24: Writing a CV	210
Chapter 25: Sending emails	216
Chapter 26: Reading papers and listening to talks	219
Chapter 27: Posters	223
Chapter 28: Giving talks	236

Chapter 29: Interviews 249
Chapter 30: Collaborating and networking 254
Chapter 31: Chairing a session at a meeting 258
Chapter 32: Chairing committee meetings 264
Chapter 33: Writing grant applications 269
Chapter 34: Other transferable skills 275

FORWARD

I recently read that the expected research career of a postdoc starting out in the 1960s was 35 years, but today it is only five. Worse, most of those postdocs will never publish a first-author paper. This means that many young scientists will never get a proper chance of a research career. Some may simply not be good enough, but many will fail because they do not understand how to make decisions that will improve their chances of doing well and how to present themselves in public.

The purpose of this book is to show scientists starting out on their career how they can give themselves the best chance of success, and how senior academics appraise graduate students and postdocs – the view, as it were, from the other side of the table. The two main sections of the book cover the postgraduate and postdoctoral years. The final section discusses transferable skills, those skills that you will be expected to have as a PhD graduate that are not specific to your research

How to Become a Scientist

work, but that are key to being seen as a professional scientist.

This book contains a great deal of information about planning a scientific career and how to deal with the inevitable problems on the way. My hope is that graduate students will use this information to make their own choices about what they want to do, where they should do it, how they should plan their future, and how to impress their elders, who may not be their betters. In short, I want them to take control of their own careers.

The perspective of the book comes from my experience as a UK academic, although my foreign colleagues tell me that graduate students face the same problems in their countries as in mine. My qualifications for writing the book are more than thirty years of training postgraduates and nine years as a principal of a four-year doctoral training programme at the University of Edinburgh, followed by three years as Director of the Graduate School of Biomedical Sciences there. I have sat through more postgraduate interviews than the proverbial dog has fleas! I became interested in postgraduate training after an unhappy period as a PhD student and could see no reason why other students should have to suffer.

Over the years, I have noted the extent to which early, sensible choices made a difference. I have seen mediocre students do well because they were focused, and brilliant students underachieve because they made bad choices, mainly because of pig-headedness. I would like to see everyone over-achieve! Being first a graduate student and then a postdoc is not easy and, if one doesn't realise what the problems can be, then it can be hard to avoid having to face them.

But how to succeed? Back in the 1960s, as a lonely graduate student in a poor lab, I bought a paperback on how to do research hoping to learn something. Today, I remember two sentences from it. The first said that research was not completed until it had been published, and the second said that nothing in the book was of any use if the reader hadn't first had a good idea. Both are, of course, keys to success and this book may help with the former, but may not be much use with the latter – apart from a few thoughts in Chapter 2 on doing research and in chapter 22 on how to be lucky (a much-underrated aspect of science). That book however said nothing on how to make the most of yourself as an up-and-coming scientist. This one tries to do just that.

Jonathan Bard
Oxford

SECTION 1

INTRODUCTION

CHAPTER 1: STARTING A CAREER IN SCIENCE

One thinks about becoming a scientist for many reasons, but particularly because one is good at it, enjoys studying it and likes the practical side of it. There is also a romantic side to uncovering Nature's secrets, although this is not something that non-scientists often appreciate. There is a joy in discovering how the natural world works and it is a privilege being part of the great journey of discovery.

If you are studying for first degree in science and are doing well, it is these thoughts that will set you off on the path of thinking about a scientific career, although you do need to know

How to Become a Scientist

that most of the subsequent reality is a bit more mundane. As you start to think about a career in science, there is an immediate set of questions that you should think about: am I sufficiently interested in it to risk three or four years of my life getting a PhD? Should I move or stay where I am? Where can I find a good lab in a University in a place where I want to live? If, in the longer term, I decide that I want an academic or research career, can I cope with the job and place insecurity? Do I take the risk of becoming so specialised that I become unemployable if the winds of science start to blow in the wrong direction?

One reassuring thing is that one can get off the research train at many stops. A useful MSc opens doors to industry, teaching and government. A PhD with a wide range of skills is also well suited for alternative careers, but they are likely to be laboratory-associated unless you make the effort to change. The difficult decisions about whether to try for a research career really crystallises once you have your PhD; this is discussed in more detail later (Chapter 17). At that stage, it is enough to say that you will need to be academically good, have published papers and have good references if you are to have a reasonable chance of success. You will also need to be lucky (Chapter 22). Subsequent advancement is difficult. For all that you may hear about the excitement of a scientific career, there are easier ways to earn a hard living!

If, however, you still like the idea of doing

science, there are no reasons not to set out on the path that leads to a PhD, if you can get funding. As more people want to do this than there are positions, the market place will soon determine whether other people think that you are up to it. The first few chapters of this book provide some keys to help you convince them, and the rest of this book assumes that you have.

As far as the public world is concerned, the job of a PhD student is to get their degree, learn laboratory and other skills, and publish some papers. There is, however, a lot more that you need to do: you have to enhance your broader abilities as much as your research ones and this means gaining transferable skills such as learning to speak in public, mastering statistics and writing well. You will also need to keep up with a much broader area of science than the very restricted domain of your own area of postgraduate research: choosing the subject for a postdoc position is the hardest choice you will have to make as it is the last time that you will be able to change research area easily. Success in your career requires that this choice takes you to an area where you see a future.

But there is a much more important task: you need to test yourself during the course of your studentship. You will have to find out if you actually enjoy doing research, even in the bad times when everything seems to be going wrong – and I hope that you will have a few of these periods. A famous physicist once told me that a PhD student whose research goes well learns nothing. This is because you need to find out if you have the resilience to cope with the times that nature seems to turn her face against you, as it certainly will. You need to decide whether you like laboratory life with its uncertain hours and if you can cope with being poorer than your undergraduate friends who seem to be on well-defined career paths and are being paid much more. It is not easy being a scientist.

The key time for this journey of internal discovery is the second year of your PhD project which may turn out to be a milestone period. This is a time when you should know the area of your research and have learnt sufficient skills to undertake substantial experiments. More important, this is likely to be the only year in your academic career when you have no other pressures. There is no thesis to work on, papers to review, grants to write, committees to sit on, students to teach or lectures to give. You can and should bury yourself in research – and you will find out a lot about yourself and what you can do. Are you original? Do you enjoy lab work that most people would rightly find dreary (the trick is to work in an area where you like the dreary bits – I liked microscopy). Do you care that the hours are unpredictable? Do you mind that you don't have much time for the rest of life? Are you resilient when things go wrong, as they invariably will? You should soon find out whether a research career is for you. If it isn't, write your thesis and move away. But be sure to produce that thesis: you will have suffered enough to have earned the title of doctor!

All of this applies to the whole of science. Is there anything special about the biosciences, my own area? Two things come to mind. First, the sheer speed with which the subject is moving as the implications of molecular technology work themselves through. The boundaries of our knowledge are probably expanding faster in the biosciences than in any subject other than computer science. Second, the downstream effects of this knowledge for industry are so great that opportunities for scientists wanting to find a job outside of academe or wanting to set up their own company have never been easier. The immediate implication of this is that any PhD student who decides that academe is not for them should take every opportunity to acquire skills that will help them in the wider world – and the better university departments provide them.

This book, however, is really aimed at those scientists who, in their hearts, want to understand more of nature. A research career is not easy, and many give up on the way as they run out of research speed and move sideways to teaching or some aspect of administration. What will carry you through the hard times is the wish to understand some aspect of the natural world – something that is yours. You may not have the clearest view of the detail now, but without that deep desire to get to grips with Nature, you will become bored. With it, you give yourself the chance of having a wonderful forty or more years making sense of the unknown.

CHAPTER 2: DOING RESEARCH

If you are thinking about a research career, you need to be clear about what you are getting into. Research is expanding knowledge and scientific research is expanding our knowledge of the natural world. Some research focuses on the detail of what we already know in outline, and theory may be particularly helpful here; other research brings the distant horizon a little closer. Some of what you will do is intended to be useful - this is applied research. Much of research, however, brings no immediate benefit, and its long-term implications may extend from nothing to world changing. The story is told of the government minister asking Michael Faraday back in the 1830s of the practical use of his experiments on electricity and magnetism and being given the reply "Why, sir, there is every probability that you will soon be able to tax it."

It is not even sensible to think of one sort

of research as being intrinsically superior to another. Who would want to rank Watson and Crick who worked out the structure of DNA and analysed its implications, Sanger who worked out how to sequence strings of amino-acids and DNA nucleotides, Brenner who, having done some of the key molecular-biology experiments in the 1960s, chose *C. elegans* as a model for studying the nervous system, and Köhler and Milstein who discovered monoclonal antibodies. They are all in the pantheon of great scientists because their work opened previously unknown doors through which other scientists could rush. What is of note in this list is that all worked at the MRC Laboratory of Molecular Biology in Cambridge, UK.

There are two lessons to be learnt from this. First, it is easier to do brilliant research in an environment where there is a culture of research expectation than anywhere else. Second, the umbrella of science is very wide and there is room under it for every sort of talent. No matter whether you are a theoretician, someone who develops techniques or an experimentalist, whether your research is pure or applied, there can be a place for you in science provided your work is good and imaginative. What you are not, at the moment, is primarily a scholar: one can imagine scholars walking along a pavement secure in their understanding the detail of what is written on the paving stones of knowledge, while research workers think about the cracks of ignorance between those stones. You do, of course, have to have some knowledge about the paving stones if you are to recognise the cracks between them, so you must keep reading. Eventually, you will be both – but you don't start out that way.

Most of the research that you will do as a graduate student will be in the nature of small steps. This is not because people want to hold you back, but because research is difficult and ground-breaking ideas are rare; indeed, even having just a good idea is hard. Einstein was once asked if he carried a notebook around with him to jot down all his brilliant ideas, and was said to have replied "No, I have so few of them". Whenever you have original ideas, cherish them and explore them: it is far better to be wrong than never to think on the greater scale, and it is better still to get into the habit of thinking about the limits of nature while you are a graduate student. Who knows where it will lead you?

What you do need to realise is that the most important research is done in your head. This may be in advance of picking up a pen, test-tube or doing anything else with your hands. All science hangs on good ideas and these can come at any time: in bed, at your desk reading, before you do experiments, while you are doing experiments, when you are looking at or analysing results, and when you are writing them up. Many people think that there is nothing like a walk for letting the mind be creative. You need to cherish your ideas whenever and wherever you have them; so, develop the ability to have them.

But having had an apparently good idea, you then need to be critical. How can you test the idea? Does the idea explain something or predict something? It is important to remember that, if an idea is not worth pursuing, it is not worth pursuing properly – you will waste time and money and lose self-confidence. Your head cannot however do its job if it doesn't have something meaty to think about. Some of this will come from the literature, but an important part comes from playing with your system so that you understand it. Small experiments designed to explore its capabilities, whatever they are, are never a waste of time.

As soon as you do start to get results in your graduate work, you need to ask yourself if they are *significant*, a word that means different things in different environments. A non-scientist will equate it with *important*, but to a scientist it means that the results *did not arise by chance* and are merely an outcome at the limits of the expectations of control observations. The key to doing good science is to realise that experimental results have to be repeatable and proven experimentally not to arise by chance through natural or experimental variation. Statistics is the branch of mathematics that deals with probability distributions and their analysis. We normally accept a result as being statistically significant if the likelihood of it arising by chance is less than 5% (p<0.05). What this means, however, is that you will be wrong in one analysis in twenty, because that is the likelihood that the result could have arisen by chance. It is better to go for a less than 1% chance (p<0.01). If you do not understand basic statistics and their use by the time you graduate with a PhD, you will have future difficulties in analysing data - don't take the risk!

There is another good way of pushing back the frontiers and that is to be lucky enough to make an observation that is counterintuitive. Many years ago, I was following up a theoretical piece of work by Alan Turing on the breakdown of symmetry in biological systems (because it was interesting, and I had some spare time). Turing said that his model, when used over a two-dimensional surface, could explain phyllotaxy, the patterning of, for example, the leaves on a stem where the clockwise and anticlockwise numbers are two successive terms of a Fibonacci sequence. He was not quite right because growth is also an important part of the process. However, some of my simulations produced stripes rather than spots and, overnight, my interest changed from plants to zebras and this led to six months of the most enjoyable work I have ever done. At the end of the book, we will discuss luck. Here, it is enough to say that you should always be on the look-out for unexpected results. You never know where they will lead, and Nobel prizes have been won because unexpected observations were followed up[1].

No matter where it leads you, don't hesitate to spread your reading and thinking across your own project, the context within which that project is situated and the major problems of your branch of science. Read widely and dream about science; it is both interesting and fun. I once heard someone dismiss research as people crawling around the frontiers of science with a magnifying glass. This is indeed a part of it, but do keep glancing up at the distant horizon.

Lovely Quote

CHAPTER 3: PLANNING YOUR CV

The reason for there being a chapter on CVs so early in this book is that it is this that will determine whether others will think that you are good enough to do a PhD and so let you start on the road to becoming a professional scientist. You may think that your CV (*curriculum vitae*, sometimes known as a resumé), the story of your academic life, represents all your achievements to date and the facts should speak for themselves when you apply for some new position. It should of course, but that is not its real role.

Although every job application requires that you submit your CV, the reality is that far too many people respond to advertisements for postgraduate, postdoc and academic positions than there are vacancies. The academics who read these CVs thus know that they will only be able to interview a small proportion of all those applicants, so their first thought on picking up yet another CV is the hope that they will find a good reason why they can reject this application, and quickly.

The truth is that *a CV has one primary purpose and that is to make the reader want to see and talk to its author*. If it doesn't do this, that CV is useless. We will take a more detailed look at how to produce as good a CV as possible in Chapter 24. Here, I want to discuss what is going on in the mind of a potential PhD supervisor or a PI thinking about filling a position (PI means *principle investigator*, someone who is responsible for a grant or is the head of a lab). Only when students know what these academics are looking for can they begin to plan the contents and structure of their CV, and so make an honest appraisal of their chances of impressing these readers. More important, if they identify gaps in their CV early enough, they can work at filling them in.

The first concern that any potential supervisor has when they appraise a CV is that the student they take on may prove to be a liability: they may not be smart enough, they may appear be passive, they may be incapable of taking control of their project or of writing up their thesis and publications (if any). Even worse, they may be a distraction to other people in the lab because they are likely to be unpleasant or, worse, they may be overdemanding of their supervisor. Your CV not only has to convince a supervisor that you are clever, but that those very real concerns do not apply to you. You may think this is all unreasonable, but you should put yourself in their position and ask what you would expect from a student if you were a potential supervisor – you would have much the same concerns.

So, when a potential supervisor picks up your CV, the first thing that they will need to do is assure themselves that you are academically up to the studentship, good enough to get funded, and the sort of person that they would positively want in their lab. Next, they will check that, while an undergraduate, you have already had some real research experience in one or more substantial laboratories during your summer vacations. This will not only mean that you know what you are letting yourself in for, but that you will already have shown a degree of commitment.

This research experience also implies that you will have something substantial to talk about in your interview beyond a final-year project that may barely be underway (see Chapter 28). If that work has led to a publication with you being a first or even a minor author, then so much the better: you will have proved that you can produce lab work of quality. It should also mean that your referees will be able to say something that carries weight - most letters of reference are pretty bland and don't help much in decision-making (unless they are bad – so make sure that your referee will support you - see Chapter 24).

Supervisors also want to know whether you

will be a good colleague, and the evidence they are looking for is that collaborative work in other labs has gone well and that you have non-scientific social interests. What they are particularly looking for, however, and very rarely find, is evidence of serious academic potential; prizes are an important indicator here. So, if your grades are good, you have worked successfully in research labs, won prizes and shown you are someone who gets on with other people, your CV should be more than good enough to get you an interview for any postgraduate studentship.

All this immediately raises two questions. First: what should you do if you don't think your CV is particularly impressive. Second, and if you have time, how can you beef up your CV. The answer to the latter question is simple: get yourself a vacation job in a lab doing something where your experience will make it worthwhile for a supervisor to take you on. Then work very hard, read assiduously and do enough to ensure that the PI of that lab will write you a good reference.

The answer to the question as to how you can give yourself an added advantage when your undergraduate CV looks a bit mediocre is also straightforward. There are two non-exclusive possibilities: first, you can postpone the decision for a year by doing an MSc or perhaps getting a job as a research assistant (the former costs, the latter pays!). This gives you a second chance at improving your academic attractiveness because you will have shown your commitment to research and gained both lab experience and transferable skills. There are actually good reasons for any student doing an MSc before their PhD. One advantage of doing so is that you will be far more sophisticated about choosing a lab and a subject for your doctoral work. Another is that you will also be able to hit the ground running in your PhD work because of your MSc experience.

The second way of getting an inside edge is to impress a potential supervisor in advance of the deadline. The simplest way of doing this is to send an email saying that you are particularly interested in one of the lab's projects and would appreciate the opportunity of a short visit to discuss an application. This email will be strengthened if you can provide a good scientific reason for your interest in that project. This visit gives the supervisor an opportunity to inspect you and it gives you the opportunity to check out the lab (see Chapter 7). The truth is that supervisors appreciate a personal interest and are far more likely to take on a student with whom they have spent time and *who has, in advance, read up about the lab and its recent publications.*

If you are applying for a postdoc position, similar rules will apply, although, if your CV doesn't show that you have used your PhD time well, you will find it hard to get a postdoc in a good lab. The key step is to contact the PI enclosing your CV explaining why you are applying for a postdoc in their lab and asking to come and see them or, if they are in a different country, to set up a skype chat. If you have good links with someone and establish a degree of trust, they are more likely to take you on than if you don't. (Thinking about where and what to do for a first postdoc is covered in Chapter 18).

In short, anyone producing a CV must appreciate what the reader will be looking for and do their best to provide it. Doing anything else is unprofessional and, if nothing else, this book is about how to become a professional.

The is one further comment to be made about CVs: they are dynamic documents and come in two versions. The obvious one sits in your computer, reflects the past and is set out as effectively as possible. The second lives in your head and should be that CV a few years down the line. This version reflects what you plan do in the next couple of years to enrich yourself as a scientist and enhance your academic profile. Do it, and don't leave your future CV to luck.

personal objectives.

CHAPTER 4: PLAGIARISM AND CHEATING

Plagiarism is claiming as your own work anything (e.g. research support, images, ideas and text) originally produced by other people; cheating is doing something dishonest that you wouldn't like others to know about. If you want to keep the good reputation that everyone starts off with, don't plagiarise or cheat. This chapter comes early in the book because it is important to understand what you must avoid doing, no matter where you are or what is your current position. Honesty is at the core of every aspect of science.

In spite of what you may have heard, almost no one commits these sins deliberately, but a few people operate at the fuzzy line between good and bad behaviour. Table 4.1 gives some examples.

Table 4.1: Plagiarism and cheating case studies

1: Do I need to thank the person who cut my sections or set up a gel – they were, after all, just minor technical tasks that anyone could have done?

2: Do I really need to thank the person who showed me which statistical analysis I needed, as I did all the actual work?

3: This experiment was done jointly with another postgraduate, but I did most of the work. Surely, I don't need to thank them in the text if they have been mentioned in the acknowledgements.

4: There is one anomalous reading in the graph of my data. Something obviously went wrong, and its inclusion is just a distraction. Surely it is sensible to just omit it.

5: My gel looks a bit fuzzy so why not improve its sharpness and contrast with Photoshop. After all, in the old days of photographs, people used the grade of paper that made the image look as good as possible.

6: My microscopic images have dust marks; surely there is no problem with removing the marks using photoshop.

7: I want to use a phrase that seems right, but someone has already used it in a published paper. Do I really need to acknowledge them?

The first two are straight plagiarism – you should thank people who helped you in the acknowledgements, and you should be explicit about the details of help. The one about statistics is particularly important: all thesis exams involve the examiners reading your thesis carefully and highlighting problems to be pursued in the oral exam, and questions about statistics are easy to pursue (why did you use this test rather than another? Is your p value too high for you to assume that Poisson analysis is appropriate?). If, under questioning, it turns out that you don't understand what you have done and why, you could find yourself being failed and told to present yourself again for another interview in three months' time; you will then be asked to prove that you understand statistics properly. Worse, if it turns out that someone else did the work and you just included it without acknowledging their work, your degree is at risk.

In the third case, you are not being honest: one way to thank a colleague properly is through an expanded acknowledgement which points to the particular experiments to which they contributed. If you don't do this, your colleague will not be pleased and your reputation in the lab will be diminished.

The fourth is cheating: if you don't like your data, redo the experiment. If you get anomalous results, don't even think of discarding them as they may reflect something important that you have been too lazy to think about. You could even miss a Nobel Prize (see chapter 2)!

The fifth is interesting: one can do a lot to enhance a photo digitally, but one needs to know the boundaries of what is appropriate. This is my view: you can do almost anything to a digital image, provided that (a) you do it to the whole image and (b) you mention what you have done in the caption. If the enhancement is more than a little contrast improvement, you may want to make a virtue of your Photoshopping by putting *before* and *after* images in your thesis. If you want to do some enhancement on a specific region of an image, you must show the before and after images and explain what you did. What you cannot do is to clean and sharpen up just a single track in a gel without showing the original image– that is cheating.

The sixth example of using photoshop to remove dust marks is interesting. There is probably little problem in doing this, provided that you are certain that the marks really are due to dust. However: some journals have an inhouse expert who checks the hidden meta-data on images and may discover that you have manipulated the image and not declared it. That discovery may cast doubt on every other image in the manuscript; it is better not to take the risk, but to clean the microscope and slide and take another image. If this is not possible, note the clean-up in the caption.

The last example is not one that would worry me in a scientific paper as the reference to the original text will certainly be somewhere in the text. Plagiarising data or an idea is a far more serious sin. If you do want to use someone else's particularly pithy phrase, it is nice to preface it with "as so-and-so (2009)" said. If, however, you are writing a non-scientific academic paper, you should know that the text-copying requirements are much more stringent.

The working rules for both plagiarism and cheating are the same. Don't do it and don't even come near to doing it. Be generous in thanking people (telling them in advance that you are doing so), in acknowledging both published and unpublished work and never, ever even think about bending the rules on cheating.

There is a cultural aspect to plagiarism that can be missed. In some countries, undergraduates are expected to copy answers from textbooks so that they know what is correct. There, this would not be seen as plagiarism, although it certainly would in postgraduate work submitted to any department across the world with normal academic standards. Everyone needs to know that, at graduate level, they are expected to use their own words and to mention the sources as references. I have seen graduate projects in which the Material and Methods section had been "borrowed" from an earlier thesis because, as the new project was a follow-on from the earlier one, the materials and methods were the same. It had to be made very clear to the student that such behaviour was plagiarism and hence unacceptable; if done again, it could cost that student their degree.

The punishments for plagiarism and cheating are that you lose your good name, risk your degree and are unlikely to get a reference that any future employer would like to receive. These risks are never worth taking.

Reporting plagiarism, cheating and other ethical concerns

The very, very occasional problem that may face you is what to do if you suspect someone else of plagiarising or cheating. It has to be said that there is no easy answer here, because you risk making yourself unpopular. Indeed, if the person is guilty and is given a deservedly hard time, you may find yourself with someone who will be antagonistic to you for a long time, and this is never comfortable.

The first thing that you should do is to tackle the problem indirectly by perhaps expressing surprise, along the lines of:

That graph doesn't look quite like the one you showed in a seminar.

Didn't so-and-so write something like that?

If you still have real worries and, in particular, think that what is happening may have an impact on the reputation of the lab, you have no choice other than to report your concerns to your supervisor. This is not a problem that you can solve by yourself.

Finally, if you have any real and strong concerns about your own or any other lab that are not solved by discussions with your supervisor (e.g. you think that animals are being badly treated), such matters need to be reported to the head of department. But you have to be prepared to risk souring the relationship with appropriate lab head (this has to be part of your conversation with the head of department).

If you do need to have such difficult conversations, you need to prepare yourself carefully, and good advice on how to do this is given by Mary Allen (*Nature*, 2019, **568**, 145).

SECTION 2

STARTING WITH AN MSC

CHAPTER 5: THE MSC YEAR

If you plan to do a PhD, there are many good reasons to do an MSc first, particularly if the funding for your doctorate only lasts for three years. The focus of your MSc should be something that you like, are good at and has a future. You will learn about a specific area of your subject at a sophisticated level, you will gain specialist lab-based and other skills, you will give yourself time to work out the direction of your career and you will be much better prepared for a PhD, in choice of both subject and laboratory. It also provides an opportunity for changing your area (e.g. a move from physics to biology or maths to physics). Finally, an MSc makes you more competitive for PhD applications.

Note: the MSc discussed in this chapter should be distinguished from the compulsory MSc that some universities require potential PhD students be registered for in their first year. If the student does badly in the first yea or changes their mind about doing a PhD, they can leave having written up an MSc thesis. If they do well, this registration is upgraded to a PhD.

There are however three groups of students who needn't do an MSc before going on to a PhD. The first are those students who know the general research problem that they want to work on for their PhD and already have some research experience. The second is those students who have done well enough as an undergraduate to get a position on a doctoral training programme (DTP) that includes an introductory, structured year during which they will do the equivalent of an MSc programme. Students on DTPs can make their choice of PhD topic a little later than those on a Masters programmes.

The third group includes students who cannot afford to take an MSc programmes. Unfortunately, this is a large group because there is very little scholarship support for MSc programmes. Perhaps the best way to get much of the experience that you would otherwise get during an MSc is to take a research-assistant job in a research lab. This will enable you to be paid while you acquire research skills and, with luck, do an interesting piece of work. This job will certainly help when you apply for a PhD because you will have shown both commitment and ability.

If you do decide to do an MSc on the way to a PhD, your first decision is where to do it. If you are already in a good university and it runs the sort of course you want to do with appropriate transferable skills support, it is practical to stay where you are. It can seem to make little sense move to a new place just for 12 months if you are then going on somewhere else.

There are however advantages to moving to a university with a higher international profile than your current one. First, it will not only look good on your CV, but will send the silent message that you are ambitious. Second, stronger universities normally run better research MSc programmes than lesser ones because they have more and better-funded research labs. Third, you will do research projects in good labs and, if you like the lab and do well in your project, you will have an advantage when it comes to applying for a PhD position there.

There are two sets of aims for an MSc (Table 5.1) and the degree of pressure that you will be under depends on whether the programme takes one or two years. If the latter, you can have a fairly relaxed first year, which will mainly require course work – you just need to do well in your assignments and exams – before the second year when the focus shifts to one or more research projects. If, however, you do a one-year Masters, the pressure starts immediately and never lifts.

For this reason, students who are comfortable about the extra year may wish to move to a country that does a two-year MSc (e.g. many of those in the European Union). There, they will find that the fees are reasonable, the course is, for better or worse, often conducted in English and they get the chance to learn a foreign language as well as seeing how a university in another country is run. There is much to be said for this, and, as you will have shown initiative and energy, it will certainly count in your favour when you apply for a PhD.

That said, there are good reasons for doing a one-year MSc which includes a long summer project and very little vacation. The intensity of the year is excellent preparation for what you should expect if you decide to do a PhD and you will be in the market for a PhD or any other job a year earlier.

Table 5.1: The reasons for doing an MSc
Public aims

1: Reach an advanced academic level in a specific area.

2: Get research experience and even publish a paper.

Private aims

3: Strengthen your CV.

4: Get a strong reference from a good lab in a good university.

5: Fill gaps in your skill base.

6: Decide if you like research enough to want to do a PhD. If so,

    Decide on the area of project that you wish to investigate.

    Decide which labs you wish to apply to.

7: Redeem an inadequate research degree

Almost everyone doing your programme will

get an MSc. Your ambition has to be to strengthen your CV during this year by achieving both the public and the private sets of ambitions in Table 5.1. You will need to do well in your courses and exams, write up good projects, impress your lecturers and supervisors and generally stand out from the rest by taking the lead in any academic activities. Expect to work very hard from day one, and this particularly applies to your research projects if you want to get that glowing references that will make a difference when you apply for a PhD.

You will probably have to make this application rather earlier than you would like if you are doing a one-year MSc. In the UK, interviews for the October intake of PhDs are often run in the previous January or February so you have to make that good impression in the first term of your Masters programme. You will thus have to decide by December whether you want to do a PhD, what you want it to be on and places you would like to do it. This means that you need to keep an early eye on the web for projects that are being advertised.

You will therefore need to do some preliminary work on the literature as soon as you have determined the specific area in which you want to do your PhD. This will mean that, once you see the advertisements, you will be able to appraise the strength of the project and of the lab. There is, it should be said, no reason why you should not email someone in whose lab you want to do a PhD with a request to visit and discuss possibilities (see Chapter 7). You should not however assume that, just because a PhD project looks good, that lab is a good place to be – this needs to be checked (Chapter 7).

MSc research projects

When you have to choose a research project, there are several things to bear in mind. First, the project should be achievable in the time allotted, even if things go slightly wrong. This probably means that it can be reduced to a straightforward question that can be experimentally or theoretically answered. Second, it should involve some skills that you already have, but allow you to develop new ones. Third, it should be in a lab where there is some immediate senior support (e.g. a postdoc). Finally, the supervisor should not be too busy to talk to you.

Once you start lab work, get into the habit of keeping good records. Keep a notebook for writing up comments and results during the day and open a file for each experiment on your PC. Write these experiments up every day in your PC and back up these records into the clouds every evening. Once you have data, analyse it statistically as soon as possible and prepare reasonable tables and graphs in Excel. Store all digital images and ensure that their identifier enables you to link them back to the details of the experiments in which they were taken. Later, you may need to reconstruct that experiment and its results for your thesis, and you do not want to encounter any problems doing this late in the year when you are under time pressure.

If things start to go pear-shaped, immediately discuss how the aims can be bent to something more achievable. You will get credit from your supervisor if you can provide evidence that the problems do not lie with you (i.e. your technical incompetence) but with the system (e.g. an antibody doesn't work or the cell-sorter has broken down) *and* you can suggest an alternative project that can be done on time. You should never assume that things will go as expected – that is the nature of research.

It is worth remembering that a negative result always reflects the question that has been asked. Nature doesn't lie, but the meaning of results is not always clear. If all your results are negative, and you trust them, try constructing the question for which these results are positive. **Hint**: *You should never assume that your original hypothesis was well-formulated.*

It sometimes happens that a project goes so well that it becomes the basis either for a stand-alone paper or as part of a bigger paper from the lab. If you really think that your work has the makings of a stand-alone paper, read Chapter 14 and have a discussion with your supervisor. If the work is complete but not enough for a paper, ask your supervisor whether it could be part of another paper. If so, make sure that you keep in contact with them, once you have left the lab. If you really like the lab and think that there is a substantial amount of further work that stems from these results, it is certainly worth considering whether you want to do a PhD on that subject in that lab with that supervisor. If and only if the answer is yes to all these questions, talk to the supervisor who may well welcome the discussion as you have shown yourself to be someone who can do research.

Writing an MSc thesis

MSc theses have to be written much more rapidly than PhD ones so, while the advice in Chapter 15 will be helpful, it needs modifying for an MSc. The easiest model for an MSc thesis is a research paper, but with a longer *Introduction* and fuller sections for *Material and Methods* and *Results*. You would, for example, be expected to include more control data and basic information about the system in a thesis than in a paper.

The simplest format for the thesis is to ask and answer a question, to formulate and test a hypothesis or to develop some technique. Under all circumstances, the *Introduction* builds up to the question, hypothesis or other aims and the *Results* end with the answer. The *Discussion* test the quality of the answer and points to future work.

If things go wrong and you don't achieve your original aim, you will need to reformulate that aim so that it meshes with the experimental conclusions that you have achieved. By doing this, you give a sense of coherence and completeness to the thesis. You may, for example, be able to answer a simpler question or hypothesis than you had hoped, or you may have clarified a question or hypothesis, or you may have discovered something unexpected. When you plan your thesis, you will need to amend your original aims so that your results show that you have achieved it (see Medawar's comments on research in Chapter 8). The point is that you will have done something positive with scientific rigour

You will inevitably run out of time and have to write up quickly. What will make this a little easier will be having your data already set out neatly in thesis-ready tables and graphs with appropriate statistical analysis. It is sensible to do this as soon as you have the results as time pressures are not so great in the middle of the project as they will be at the end. If you have to repeat the experiment, you will then already know how to do it and how to set out the results graphically, so things should go rapidly. It should go without saying that you should keep a good notebook on your computer in which all details of your work have been written up on the day that it was done.

Behaviour in a lab
You cannot hide in a lab: everyone around you

will soon know if you are working hard, turning up regularly, progressing well
or being idle, and whether you have green fingers or are technically incompetent. You will start off with people wanting you to do well, so keep them on your side by being seen to be enthusiastic, being willing to do your share of any communal lab work and in due course being helpful to others. If people like you, they will be more than willing to help you if things go wrong with your experimental work. Get into the habit of keeping your bench area and equipment tidy and clean, even if you are naturally untidy! If others see a messy work area when you are not in the lab, you will create a bad impression. If your reference says that you were a pleasure to have in the lab, so much the better!

If you have use of a desktop computer and you use it for non-work purposes, make sure that you log out when you are not in the lab. I still recall the occasion when a technician moved a mouse on a computer that had been used by graduate student. The PC woke up to display pornography and I had to sort out the offence that this caused.

Even if your supervisor is not there very often, labs are places where gossip is rife, and they will soon hear what impression you are making on the rest of the lab. This will matter when you want a reference.

CHAPTER 6: THINKING ABOUT A PHD

If you are doing well in your undergraduate or MSc science course or have worked successfully in industry for a year or two, you will naturally be thinking about doing a PhD. You should however be aware that embarking on a long postgraduate course carries risks. You are unlikely ever to be more than adequately paid unless you move out of academe and acquire some managerial skills. You will never catch up financially with those of your friends who are intending to do an MBA or the like. You will have to work hard and for long hours. You may have to move several times over the coming decade and have an unclear, insecure future for longer than you might like. You may well be lonely as you move to new places where you initially don't know anyone, although spending long periods thinking and writ-

How to Become a Scientist

ing on their own is something most academics see as natural and even enjoyable.

There are, I am glad to say, a set of benefits to balance these downsides. You will get to find out if you really like doing science, and most of us do. You will have a considerable degree of freedom in your working life together with opportunities for travel. You are likely to develop an international group of friends and, if things go reasonably well, have an enjoyable if hard-working career. Only you can decide if the goods outweigh the bads.

If, at the end, you decide that academe is not for you, there are many alternatives to move to where your skills will be respected and these include industry, the scientific side of the civil service, journalism, patent work and teaching (Chapter 20). One of the side benefits of doing a PhD, other than being called doctor for the rest of your life, is that you can spend a few years doing research in an interesting environment working out what it is that you would really enjoy doing for your long-term future.

The aim of a PhD training is to teach you how to do research and to build up your professional expertise in your subject of choice. You may naturally want to get a PhD in your own country for language reasons alone. What you will however find is that, across international academe, much of the work is done in English, which is now the natural language of scientific research. The upside for those whose first language is English is that this makes things easy; the downside is that they can get away with being monoglot. English is my first language and, even for me, it is not easy to write colloquial English prose. I therefore have considerable sympathy with non-native speakers who have to learn to read, write and speak a difficult foreign language. I would only say that, the sooner you get to grips with written scientific English, the better for your future career. If you have any doubts about your linguistic ability, ensure that the university to which you apply for a PhD both expects you to work in English and runs good language courses.

There is a spectrum of PhD styles, and different countries have different expectations. The simplest doctorate is the traditional UK PhD: this just requires that you spend three years doing some research and writing it up in a thesis (no publications are required). The two advantages of this are that you get into the swing of doing research very young and you can start to earn a proper living sooner than under any other system. The disadvantages are that your knowledge may be a bit narrow, you may not finish on time and be poor when your grant runs out. In addition, you take a risk in your choice of project: because you are unlikely to know the area of research well before you start, you have to depend on your supervisor for the details of the project and how to get started – and supervisors can be wrong. At least things in the UK are now much better than they

How to Become a Scientist

used to be as you no longer have supervisors saying: "find yourself something to do; if you can't, you shouldn't be doing a PhD".

Although some students in the UK do three-year PhDs, many departments now have four-year doctoral training programmes (DTPs), with students doing a preliminary year of full-time training before embarking on the research for their PhD. In this first year, which may be awarded an MSc, students will do some course-work, learn some transferable skills and do some research projects that have to be written up to MSc standards. Around the middle of the year and on the basis of the PhD projects available, students will choose a lab for their doctoral work, and it is often one of those in which they have done projects.

The advantage of the DTP system is that students have sufficient experience to make an informed choice of PhD project, will have enough research experience and technical experience to get started and should be able hit the ground running. In this system, there is little excuse (other than that research can go wrong) for not completing the work for the thesis, writing it up and at least sending papers for publication within the remaining three years for which there is funding. In spite of all these advantages, some DTP students still don't finish on time.

The system in continental Europe is similar, but tends to be structured around the Bologna Process. Perhaps the first difference from postgraduate work in the UK is that the Bologna-style MSc tends to take two years (with a long summer break) rather than one; students learn a little more and their life is less pressured. You need to know, however, that pressure comes with research and academic life and the sooner you get used to it the better. The second difference is that most counties in continental Europe demand published papers before the PhD thesis is submitted. In Scandinavia, your PhD thesis is your set of papers bounded by an introduction and a discussion. (It is possible to submit such a thesis in the UK, but I have only come across it twice.) This means that a PhD may take longer than you might wish.

Things are slightly different in the USA mainly because having a PhD carries implications of a professional qualification as much as a research one. If you do an MSc before your PhD, you can expect your postgraduate education to take at least 6 years, while few who go straight to a PhD after a first degree would expect to complete in less than five years. For this, you would spend your first 18 months or so studying a broad range of topics for your prelims exam and these are notoriously tough. During this period, you usually take a lab-based project.

Once you pass the prelims, you can start your thesis work, and your income may now be supplemented by part-time paid teaching. The upside of this system is that USA PhDs from good labs really are professionals. The downsides are that they may not complete their thesis until their late twenties, that they run out of energy and money and that life in the form of partners and children starts to demand that they earn a proper income before writing up. Only in the USA is the ABG (All But Dissertation) recognised!

My own view is that you should try and get through the PhD as soon as is possible and start to earn a proper living. If you don't complete on time, you will be poor, and this is never a good thing. You also need to get your degree from as impressive a lab and institution as possible: this will not only add kudos to your CV, but will help ensure that you make a good academic network of friends and colleagues, one that will lubricate your future career.

Getting started

You will have to decide what sort of PhD position you prefer. In my view, your first choice, if you are certain that you want to do a PhD in the UK, should be to aim for a DTP which provides four years of stable training. These are unfortunately very competitive. If you are not sure about your future or you have limited research experience or you want to redeem a mediocre first degree, you should go for an MSc or possibly a research-assistant job to get that research experience and to develop your academic skills. This year has the advantage that you will be able to make a far more informed choice of your research topic and lab than you can as a final-year undergraduate. Equally important, it gives you the opportunity to decide whether you really want to spend all that time working on a PhD. If you don't, then you can get off the academic escalator easily with an MSc degree and some research experience to prove that you have used your time profitably.

If you have a good idea of the general area in which you are interested in doing a PhD (and you should), you should approach someone in your own university and ask them for advice. This conversation will go better if you have already done some homework on the literature. With luck, this conversation will lead to some useful suggestions. You can also search on the web either at general sites like findaphd.com (which also includes a great deal of well-written general information) or on the sites of any university department which has a good reputation in your chosen area. Finally, of course, you can use Google. What you will be looking for in these advertisements are interesting projects in a good university for which there is a good chance of funding.

CHAPTER 7: CHOOSING A LAB AND A SUPERVISOR FOR A PHD

How can you tell whether a university will provide a good PhD education? In one sense, you will never the know the answer until you have the degree and have been able to move on to a good postdoc position. There are, however, pointers, and these cover the department, the laboratory, the project, the supervisor and of course funding. This chapter gives you some of them.

Doing a PhD is an expensive business as there are costs for university fees and for your lab work, not to mention what you will need for living. Very few people can afford to pay for their own postgraduate training or find it practical to take out loans. (***Hint***: *do not apply for anything for which* *there is no chance of funding.*) Instead, look for advertisement offering studentships for you are eligible; you can then decide whether your CV is good enough to make you competitive for them. If in doubt, discuss the matter with someone in your department.

If you are determined to do a PhD, apply to every lab doing work in which you are interested, remembering that your letter of application needs to convince the lab head that you are a serious applicant. Once a lab shows some interest in you, your job is to vet it (Table 7.1), and decide if having been there and at that university is likely to be a positive experience and will enhance your CV.

A word of warning: Be careful about applying for a PhD at an institution that does not have a good number of postgraduate students or whose website fails to provide details of postgraduate training and support. Also be careful with labs where you would be the only graduate student. An example would be the lab of a newly appointed academic. Apart from the risk that you may waste 6 months while the lab gets going, you may find yourself isolated with no other graduate students to talk to or collaborate with. If you are considering such a position, make sure that there is a nearby lab with similar interests which does have graduate students in which you can get going and that your potential supervisor has funding in place to cover your research costs.

As soon as you identify a possible lab and project, ask around your own department to see if other people in its area have heard of it. "No" is not a good answer here! You should then explore its departmental website to look for the structure of its postgraduate education and the support it gives to students. What you are looking for are opportunities to do transferable-skills courses and details on how supervision and support are provided.

In my department at Edinburgh University, students answered to a small committee of a main supervisor, a second supervisor, who was usually from another lab, and a chair who was normally someone older and more experienced who could keep an informal eye on progress and was a neutral contact in case of problems with supervisors. We prided ourselves on providing good support for our students. In my department in Oxford, all postgraduates are assigned to a group where they can give talks to one another. A good pointer of a strong postgraduate culture is is the presence of a webpage or Facebook page devoted to and run by the departmental postgraduates.

Next, look at the web page for the lab and see how big it is as you need to sense where you would feel comfortable. Large labs are very structured with postdocs, postgraduates and technicians, there may also be a lab manager. If you are not a reasonably outgoing character, you may get lost in these. Smaller labs with just a postdoc and a couple of students may not provide all the technical resources that some research needs, but some people feel far more at home in these more modest surroundings, particularly if there are other larger labs in the department that can provide wider support. You need to find an environment that suits you.

Also on the lab website will be lists of grants, recent publications and information about lab meetings and other social events. It can be difficult being in a lab which is poorly funded so check that the lab is receiving regular grants. The publication list is important because it tells you both if the lab is research-active and whether it collaborates with other labs (including those in other countries). The supervisor's publications (accessible via PubMed and similar databases), which you should read before making an application, will also tell you if the students in the lab are publishing their work and so getting credit. You do not want to be in a lab whose students don't write papers. Neither do you want to be in a lab that doesn't have regular lab meetings and seminars.

Finally, you need to find out as much as possible about the potential supervisor. It has to be said immediately that any supervisor worth having is not likely to have enough time to supervise you closely. Good academics are unreasonably busy giving lectures, attending meetings, reviewing papers, writing grant applications, running their lab, writing papers, teaching undergraduates and attending committee meetings. Postgraduate students come last. In such labs, the best that you can hope for is for your supervisor to give you a starting project and to see you regularly, but probably not frequently (see Chapter 10 on how to handle your supervisor). Your day-to-day supervision will probably be in the hands of a postdoc. This is not a bad thing because experienced postdocs are usually masters of techniques and are ambitious to write papers. If they help you, they will get their name on your papers and hence add credit to their CVs so the relationship is mutually helpful.

Once you have made serious contact with a lab, you should try to visit it – or at least have a skype conversation with the lab head. This visit is particularly important if your CV is not particularly good, as it gives you a chance to impress the potential supervisor in advance of the deadline. Your request will be strengthened if you can provide a good scientific reason for your interest in that project (e.g. *I came across a particular paper that interested me because* …). This visit gives the supervisor an opportunity to inspect you and perhaps give you the benefit of the doubt. The truth is that supervisors appreciate a personal interest and are far more likely to take on a student with whom they have spent time and who can talk sensibly about their work. **Hint**: *Whenever you visit a PI, read up, in advance about their lab and its recent publications.*

Table 7.1: A check list for vetting labs
1: Is the lab the right size?
>A lab with a postdoc, technician and 2 PGs is probably fine, but it should have links to other labs.
>
>if larger, you may get lost unless you are "noisy".
>
>if smaller or isolated, it may be short on technical and colleague support.

2: Are you encouraged to talk to the lower levels, particularly PGs?

3: Is the lab well-funded (and how long does the funding last)?

4: Who would be a second supervisor and what would s/he have to offer?

5: Who would supervise you on a day-to-day basis?

6: Are there regular talks, lab meetings, seminars etc?

7: Does the lab produce a solid output of papers?

8: Does the lab seem like a pleasant place to be?

9: What does the grapevine (e.g. PG students) say? *You must find out*

10: Are there transferable skills courses on offer?

11: Does the supervisor have colleagues and collaborations? If any of these questions yield a "no/poor" answer, be worried!

During this conversation, you might ask for details of a student that you could have a chat with. This is by far the best way of finding out what life in the lab is really like for graduate students. What you want to know is how things go on a day-to-day basis, whether there are regular journal clubs and lab meetings and whether they feel that they are adequately supervised with the support or availability of a second supervisor. As a result of this conversation you will sense whether the graduate students seem relaxed and welcoming and whether the lab feels like a place in which you would be comfortable.

Do not press the person you are talking to as they are very unlikely to say that life is dreadful. You should question them very gently and in a relaxed way. Remember that, while you are forming an opinion about them and the lab, they are forming one about you too – and you may become colleagues in six months' time.

Note that, although it was the project that drew you to the lab, this hasn't been mentioned yet. The truth is that the overt project that you start with is unlikely to be the one you end with, unless a lot of preliminary work has already been done. In this case, the project may be so well-defined that it needs very little thinking and any competent technician could do it: for you it would only be a means of getting going in the lab. Acting as a technician is not what doctoral training is about: you need something sufficiently ill-defined that you get to see if you like working on the unknown as well as the known – this is the topic of the next chapter.

Studentships in good labs are competitive and, no matter how good you are or how shy you are, you will need to apply to several labs, more than you might think. They have to want you and you have to want them. If you get a sense that one is not right for you, try elsewhere. You only get one shot at a PhD and you need to give yourself the best possible chance of things going right.

SECTION 3

THE PHD YEARS

CHAPTER 8: CHOOSING A PHD RESEARCH PROJECT

Although supervisors may give you a topic title and an abstract and the department that interviews you may expect you to expand this into a project proposal, do not think that this is precisely what you will be doing for the next three years. Nature tends not to be that obliging!

The reality is that you first choose an area of research that interests you and then look for a project in or near it. Somewhat surprisingly, the details of the project do not actually matter too much: what you require is a topic where something is known, but there is also room for you, through reading, thinking and experimentation or theoretical analysis, to explore what is not known. Your aims should be to work in an area where you can learn a lot and do a lot so that, at the end of three years or so, you are on your way to having a deep knowledge of your area of science and confidence in both your technical skills and your research abilities.

Insofar as there is a trick to getting a PhD, it is realising that your thesis will have to include several research chapters each of which can be seen as asking a question and answering it (a theme returned to in Chapter 15 when we discuss how to write a thesis). A good project topic is one that allows you to ask linked questions which you will be able to answer through careful analysis followed by a fair amount of lab work using a wide variety of techniques (learning these is an important part of a doctoral education). If the area doesn't appear to lend itself to this breadth, then you need to be prepared to broaden the topic. If this concerns you, you shouldn't immediately run to your supervisor for advice, but work out for yourself what needs doing. Then is the time for that discussion with your supervisor.

You should not expect these questions to come to you immediately and you should also not assume that the questions you set out to answer are the ones that you will end up answering. Professor Sir Peter Medawar (1915-1987), who won a Nobel prize for immunology and who wrote widely about the philosophy of science, is interesting here. In his talk "*Is the scientific paper a fraud*?", he argued that it is not that papers contain wrong data but that their logic is back-to-front.

The paper typically starts by giving the question that it seeks to answer, explains how the investigation will be done, gives the results of that investigation and, in the discussion establishes the answer.

This, Medawar claims, is not how science is done. The reality is that a scientist interested in answering a particular question begins by exploring the system; some of the experimental results are interesting, most are not. They then probe the interesting results further and slowly some understanding emerges, and this is clarified through further work. It is only at this stage that one can identify the precise questions whose answers can clarify what is going on. Only then can one do the key experiments that of course provide the answers already indicated by the preliminary work. These final experiments are of course the only ones that are published. The resulting paper never reflects the reality of the full story because it starts with a question and ends with an answer, whereas the actual work started with that answer and worked back to the question.

The lesson that one takes from Sir Peter, who was a brilliant experimentalist, is that one cannot do good experimental work until one has understood one's experimental system in real depth. Doing this is the first step in all new projects. You may think that the literature will tell you all you need to know, but you will be wrong. If you look at a well-understood, but complex system with, for example, a new technique, it is highly likely that you will observe something new, and something new is what you want to discover.

This is not to say that you should ignore the advice of your supervisor, the postdocs in your lab and the literature. You must use this advice as a baseline, but you must learn to explore things for yourself. If you do not really understand how your system operates, you are unlikely to appreciate or even notice experiments that modulate the normal response. You will need to master and develop assays that allow you to identify change; learning to take scientific responsibility for your project is a necessary part of your doctoral training.

So, when you see a project title and summary that has been advertised, do not accept it passively, but read about it and think about it. Are there obvious, straightforward questions that can be asked? Is so much known about the system that all your PhD work will do is fill in gaps in existing knowledge or does it hold the potential of giving you a serious look into the unknown? You of course want to get a PhD, but you also need to develop your scientific abilities; for this, unexplored territory is where you will want to spend at least some of your time as a graduate student. Make sure that your project is not too precisely defined.

CHAPTER 9: THE FIRST YEAR OF A PHD

A month or so before you intend to arrive in your new lab, you should contact your supervisor to let them know when you expect to arrive and ask them to suggest a few important papers that they recommend that you read. You should also ask whether there is anything else that you should do before you arrive in addition to any paperwork that the University or Department has sent you. You will of course also need to find accommodation and the easiest way to do this, other than to follow the advice of the accommodation office, is to ask the supervisor for the names and email addresses of other PhD students in the lab and contact them to see if they can help. If it is possible, it is better to do all this during a visit.

You will have arrived at your new university a

week early, arranged accommodation (preferably in a shared flat so that you start off with a social group who will be outside of the lab), done all the basic administrative paperwork and arranged a time to meet your new supervisor. When you walk in to your new lab for that meeting (with a notepad because you will never remember everything that you will have been told), you need to have some ideas as to what you want out to discuss. Table 9.1 gives some suggestions.

Table 9.1: Topics for a first meeting with a supervisor

1: A general discussion about your project.
2: Ideas for an initial project to get going.
3: How the lab works (*some of this may come from a technician or a postdoc*).
Who is responsible for administration and equipment? How are consumables and equipment ordered?
4: Will you have a second supervisor and will they be in another lab?
5: A suggestion as to who might mentor you as you get going in the lab (this should be a senior graduate student or a postdoc).
6: What skill and other courses should be done and whom should you approach about them.
7: What administrative hurdles need to be jumped.
8: Who is the head of the postgraduate studies committee (you will need to introduce yourself to them)? Hopefully, they will have a get-together for all the new postgraduate students.

9: Anything else that needs to be done by you or by anyone else.

10: Anything else that you want to know.

Your relationship with your supervisor inevitably starts off on a slightly formal basis as you do not know one another, but it should soon relax. As your supervisor will be the key person in getting you through your PhD and writing your future references, you should work hard at this relationship. You should learn to distinguish between working meetings and informal chats (e.g. at coffee breaks) which, on the science side ,should never go much beyond "can we get together next week to talk about whatever" or "could you spare a moment to look at a result". If you want to talk about something serious with your supervisor, you should make an appointment for a working meeting. It is best that such meetings with your supervisor should be business-like and planned.

It is important to have a clear idea of what you want to achieve in your first year and a list is given in Table 9.2, although you might want to amend it in the particular light of your own programme. The key thing is to have a list so that you can be sure, as the year goes by, that you are on track.

Table 9.2: Some aims for the first year of a PhD

1: Getting going in the lab and learning how it works.

2: Doing appropriate courses on advanced topics in your area and on transferable skills, particularly

How to Become a Scientist

statistics and programming. If you are a theoretician, formal courses in advanced mathematical and programming topics may well be compulsory.

3: Attending seminars and journal clubs (you should soon be presenting papers).

4: Getting involved in general postgraduate activity.

5: Doing a small but easy project and writing it up. This should be done within six months.

Doing this is key to learning about your system.

6: Learn some new techniques.

7: Jumping through whatever administrative and other hoops that the department demands.

8: Developing your ideas for the thesis. You should have the beginnings of clear ideas by the end of your six-month project.

Try to articulate some key questions that link to a single theme.

Identify the techniques that handling them will require.

Do the preliminary reading to know how others have approached the questions.

Include one aim that will be easy to achieve (to get you through hard times!),

Some ideas should be of limited ambition; others shouldn't.

Getting research work started

How do you get going on your PhD research? Some people like to start by conducting a detailed literature research of everything has been published on their topic, and only get to the lab once they feel confident that they are on top of it all. This is not a sensible approach because you will get overwhelmed with information that you can't properly appreciate because you don't know enough about the system.

It is far better to start with reading just the core literature and focus on immediate lab work aimed at getting a sense of the phenomenon that you will investigate. It is only when you have had hands-on experience of the system will you be able to read the research literature critically. Even more important, perhaps, is that weighing your mind down with the literature before you have a practical sense of the system makes it hard to think originally.

What gives this early lab work a focus is to base it around a simple, straightforward project with limited aims that should take, including writing it up, no more than about 6 months. This project may be suggested by your supervisor, may be part of a bigger project involving other lab members (this is the best choice because it will enable to become a natural part of lab life if you are new to the lab) or you may have to produce it for yourself.

Doing such a project carries several immediate benefits. First, you will get used to the lab; second, you will have to develop your skills in using an important set of techniques, some of which should be new; third you will develop your

How to Become a Scientist

intuitions about the system, be it an organism, an in vitro system, molecular genetics, a complex organic molecule, or something more physical. The key thing is that you should not only get some results, but use them to answer some research question. Do this and you are on your way to becoming a successful research student.

If you did a Masters project in this lab, you may feel that you can jump straight to a rather more substantial project. This is probably not a good idea as everyone's self-confidence benefits from an early success. However, because you already have a good sense of the system, your best choice is to use this opportunity to ask a question whose answers need techniques that are new to you and that will be useful in the future and whose use will help you understand more about your system.

You will inevitably spend a great deal of time in your lab and should always remember that it is a place of work so behave properly. Always keep your bench tidy and, initially at least, ask for consumables rather than taking them. You should discover how the lab works, how purchasing is handled and signed for, who runs which pieces of equipment and who is responsible on a day-to-day basis for the lab as a whole. Equipment maintenance may be on a rota basis and you will be expected to be part of it. Learn to respect technical expertise and the people who have it – you may need their help and people are much more willing to provide this to people that they like. Time spent in learning to be a good citizen will soon pay for itself.

Keeping good lab notes and files

The discipline that you needed for a Masters project (last chapter) is even more important for a PhD. First set up a proper structure of folders on your computer so that every aspect of your work has a natural slot (references, images, spreadsheets etc., and make sure you know how to link them). You should also keep a lab notebook for writing comments as you go. Get into the habit of writing up your work on a daily basis – it is very easy to forget exactly what you have done that day, what results you have got, what problems you have encountered and what good thoughts have passed through your mind.

Writing up your results

Once you have done sufficient lab work to get the results that answered your initial question, you should write it up. Ideally, this will be in the style of a paper intended for publication, with properly set out graphs, tables and images, together with any statistical analysis needed. It should however differ from a paper in three ways. First, you should include more baseline data than would normally be included in a publication. Second, there should be a section on chance observations of interest. Third, you should include in the discussion a section along the lines of implications for future research.

Once this has been done, you should make an appointment with your supervisor and send them a print out of the write-up so that they can annotate it. They will need a reasonable amount of time to read what you have done so you shouldn't expect the appointment to be offered for the following day. When you do meet, you would expect to discuss how the proposal looks, how it could be improved and what you should do next, all with an eye to formulating a detailed PhD proposal. (This is irrespective of whether you were asked to do one before you came. You are now in a far better position to produce something realistic). The job of the supervisor is to read this proposal critically, so you may not be congratulated to the extent that you were hoping.

While you are doing all this, you also need to keep up with the literature, work on acquiring transferable skills and starting to use them. You also need to find out about talks, journal clubs, lab meetings, how the lab works and get to know a wide range of people. If the lab has technicians, get to know them as you will need their help. You will be extremely busy, but you should not only have enjoyed all this effort, but you will have learnt a lot, done a lot and got some results. With luck, you will also have been to a few interesting seminars. In short, you will now feel at home in your new lab and department.

Once this project is completed, you will need

to start work on a thesis plan for the rest of this year and for the next. This will particularly include the initial draft of the questions that your PhD intends to answer, and you might like to glance at Chapter 15 which discusses how to write a thesis. The path is easier to negotiate if you know where it is going to end.

These questions should not be too tightly drawn for two reasons. First, you may not have asked questions that are easy to answer. Indeed, it may turn out to be impossible to answer them precisely. Second, each question needs to be loose enough to allow for the possibility of unexpected observations that may lead you into interesting areas. It is likely that your department will expect to see your thesis plan and you may also have to defend it. It really is worth putting considerable effort into producing it.

If things have not gone according to plan

If you have done everything in Table 9.1 and it has all worked, you will have done well and earned your summer holiday! Many students will feel however feel that the year has not gone as well as they had hoped. The course work was too hard or was a waste of time, the initial project has not been as productive as hoped for, a new technique that should have been straightforward wasn't, relationships with some of the people in the lab have been difficult, or there have been periods of loneliness or other emotional stresses. Indeed, most graduate students go through periods when things feel wrong. Some of these problems together with their possible solutions are discussed in Chapter 13 and you should read it if you feel that they apply to you, if only to realise that you are not alone.

Here I want to mention two particularly serious problems that are interrelated: depression and the wish to run away. Everyone goes through ups and downs at work; depression is when it affects your physical and mental health. You may not be able to sleep, or you can't stop sleeping, your appetite may swing one way or the other, or you may feel hopeless and generally low. If you are in this state, you may be suffering clinical depression and you need medical help. Please go to the university health centre as soon as possible; they will have a great deal of experience in helping people like you because many students unfortunately get depressed. The very great majority do however recover as this sort of reactive depression goes away when things get better.

The other problem for now is what to do when, over a period of weeks, you begin to feel that it was all a terrible mistake and research is not for you. Here, you will have to distinguish between the possibility that you hate it because nothing is working, as opposed to that you are bored, don't care one way or the other and wish that you were doing something (anything) else. In either case, you should first speak to your supervisor who may be able to give you extra support or realise that your first project was too ambitious or that something technical was awry. A little success in the lab may be enough to make you realise that you had just been reacting to lab failure.

If, in the cold light of day after having persisted a little longer, you really do think that lab life is not for you and you would rather take an alternative path, then perhaps you should. It is however not sensible to walk away with nothing as what can be seen as failure does not look good on your CV, even if the reasons are good.

Before you make any irreversible decisions talk things through with your supervisor or the head of the departmental postgraduate committee. The discussion may help clarify your mind one way, or the other. If you do decide you should go, it is both good manners and sensible for you to do so in an orderly way (it may also be the best way to get a good reference!). Whatever happens, you owe an obligation to your supervisor and their lab as they have provided you with a home for the best part of a year and have funded your work. The thing to do is to set up a meeting with your supervisor, explain the situation and work through all the problems. Do not make any decisions at this meeting, but leave things for a week to settle your mind.

If you then feel that you need to leave, discuss the best way of doing this with your supervisor. You might, for example, ask about the possibilities of doing an MSc before you go so that you will get a qualification that will useful when you apply for a job elsewhere, while the lab will have a piece of completed work that they can include in a future publication or grant application. If you already have an MSc, then work out what you want to do next before going public: you may be able to use your remaining time to do some course work or some reading that will help in your new career. While doing this, you may be able to do something worthwhile with the work that you have done; it could, for example, contribute to another ongoing project in the lab. The reference from your supervisor will be far better for you if they can say that you left having been helpful and good in the lab rather than that you walked out because you were an unreasonable person who wasn't much use at research.

If you are going through a hard time, do try to work your way through it. Every student wants their research to go well and to get their PhD on time, with no serious problems. But there will always be problems and you will learn a great deal from them so don't sink under their weight. By confronting difficulties and overcoming them, you develop strength, resilience and confidence. In the limits, the one good reason for leaving early is that you know, in your heart of hearts after serious introspection and discussion with others that research is not for you.

A personal note may be helpful here. I initially had a very bad time as a graduate student with a supervisor who turned out not to be much interested in or good at research. In June of my second year, I ran away for three months because I had done nothing of any use and was severely depressed. I was however allowed back in October, decided on some projects that I thought I should be able to do and submitted my thesis 16 months later having published two papers. I was first unlucky and then lucky – such is the way of the world.

CHAPTER 10: HANDLING SUPERVISORS

No matter whether you are doing a small project, an MSc project, a PhD or a postdoc, much of its success will inevitably depend on your supervisor(s), so your relationship with them is something that you need to get right[2]. At its base, you will start by needing support from them for ideas, lab facilities and discussion; later you will need help with writing up, while you will end by needing a reference and perhaps collaborating in future work and in writing papers. If you get things right, you will also have a long-term mentor, colleagues and friend.

The relationship is asymmetric: your supervisor would like to see you as someone who will initially need a lot of academic and financial support, but will pay the lab back by doing good quality and useful work. Anything else that they get is a bonus, although having successfully supervised a PhD student, particularly one who has produced publications is always good for their CV. Moreover, although you are but a secondary part of their academic and research work; they are key to yours. Your supervisor is thus more important to you than you are to them, and the onus is on you to make the relationship work, particularly at the beginning when you are getting going.

All this does not mean that you are a technician to do what you are told. A key part of being a graduate student or a postdoc is learning to take the initiative and become independent. You should end up not needing your supervisor. It is you who will be examined on your thesis, not your supervisor. Understanding the dynamics of the student-supervisor relationship makes handling it easier. In general, the supervisor should be seen as more of an advisor than a boss, although you are clearly a junior member of the lab.

First, you need to realise that anyone good enough to run the sort of lab you want to work in is going to be very busy indeed with undergraduate teaching, writing papers and grants applications, reviewing papers and sitting on committees. While their research work is of course important, it has to be fitted in to all their other immediate commitments. It is therefore inevitable that, on the great scale of things, time for postgraduates will come after their own experiments, analysing their results and time spent with

How to Become a Scientist

their postdocs.

Second, you should appreciate that you will not get to spend long periods with your supervisor, and you have to make the most of the time that you are alone with them.

Third, you will need to work on producing your own support networks for day-to-day survival. These will ideally include a second supervisor, who should be from another lab, the people in your own lab (postdocs, technicians and other graduate students) and graduate students from the wider department. This requirement for mutual support is one of the reasons why there needs to be a strong postgraduate culture in your department. You should also know who is the chair of the departmental postgraduate studies committee (CPGSC) as it is they who oversee all graduate administration. If things go wrong, or the relationship between you and your supervisor breaks down, as very occasionally happens (see Chapter 13), this committee will have to sort things out. You should introduce yourself to the chair soon after you arrive so that they at least know who you are.

Finally, you should remember that supervisors are human too! They can get bad news, things can go wrong for them, they can be ill. All of this means that they can have bad days in the same way that you can. Adults need to be able to make allowances for one another so, if things don't go well on some occasion, bring things to a halt and try another day. You could, for example, say that your supervisor has given you something to think about and perhaps further discussion could be postponed until you have done another experiment or worked through the implications of today's discussion.

As to how you should call your supervisor, most labs are fairly informal, and almost everyone is on first-name terms. You do no harm in your first meeting by referring to your supervisor as Doctor or Professor and see if you are invited to use their first names. If you are, but are not accustomed to being on first-name terms with senior people, do not assume that this informality means that you are equals!

Further meetings with your supervisor

These, which should be regular but not necessarily frequent, are of two sorts: informal meetings over coffee or in the lab and more formal meetings in your supervisor' office. The former are not really for discussing serious matters, the exception being when your supervisor sees you in the lab and asks about some result or how things are going. Let the supervisor take the initiative here.

Interactions with your supervisor are rather easier in a small lab than a big one as the supervisor has proportionately less time for each member of the lab in the latter. Even so, it can sometimes be hard to get your supervisor's attention. So, if you want to see your supervisor about something substantial, you should email them asking for a meeting saying why, even if it is only to sign some piece of paperwork. If it is to show them something you have written, you should attach it to the email; if that text is more than a few pages then the meeting is likely to take some time, so you should expect a reply of "next week" rather than "drop by after coffee".

The general rule is that you should not try to cover too much in one meeting. Even if the meeting is arranged after an informal chat in the lab, it is usually sensible to follow this up with a confirmatory email; this will remind your supervisor to put the details in their diary. Although you shouldn't bother your supervisor about trivial things, it is important that you keep in regular contract with them. In general, students who go for long periods without making contact are generally of greater concern to supervisors than those who make excessive demands.

You need to be aware that, if you manage your supervisor well, they will feel that you are a serious, professional, well-organised person who only bothers them when they should be bothered. In practice, this means that you should plan meetings carefully and keep good notes of what they have said. This will allow you to say things like "Picking up on last time when you suggested that I come back once I had done .....".

You should at the least set up meetings with your supervisor when you start and end particular pieces of work. Supervisors like results, particularly those with good pictures properly annotated and graphs and tables with statistical analysis. The only times that you should show incomplete work to your supervisor is when something really isn't working and you need their technical expertise, or when you have discovered something interesting (and repeatable) that you think that they would like to know about.

If you get the structure of your meetings right, your supervisor will appreciate your only coming to see them when you have a good reason. This good impression means that, if things are not going well for some reason, you will get the benefit of the doubt. But beware: if you are having problems in the lab, these cannot be kept private: labs are places where gossip is rife, and supervisors will soon hear what the rest of the group thinks of you. It is always better if your supervisor associates you with good news!

When it comes to writing up (see Chapter 15), there are two rules. First, never show scruffy first drafts to your supervisor and, second, don't ask them to read too much in advance of the meeting. I remember the supervisor who complained to me about the student who emailed them saying "I am expecting to submit my thesis early next week so could you please read it all through and let me have any final comments by Monday". This email was sent on the previous Wednesday and was opened by their supervisor at Heathrow airport (London) on their way to a meeting in New York. The supervisor did not meet the student's deadline!

Second supervisors

Many universities require PhD students to have a second supervisor for several reasons. First, they and their lab provide another set of contacts. Second, there is another senior member of staff with an interest in you and who may also be able to write you a reference. Third, they and their lab will introduce you to another, related area of research and perhaps additional technology. Finally, you will have a back-up home should things go wrong (and I emphasise that this only happens very occasionally).

If no second supervisor is appointed at the beginning of the project, there is no urgency in making a choice, so you might leave the subject for a month or two before raising it with your supervisor. If there is no obvious person for the role, they may suggest that your second supervisor should be a senior postdoc in the lab. This is not a good idea in general, partly because a postdoc cannot be really independent of their PI and partly because postdocs often move on and this may be before you complete. Moreover, because they are more available than your supervisor, you will get the benefit of their help irrespective of their status. It may be better to reply that you were hoping for someone from another lab because of the additional technical support that they could offer. If no sensible suggestion is forthcoming, then it is best to suggest leaving the matter for a week.

This will give you time to discover someone for yourself, having seen who else is in the department who runs a good lab that is complementary to your own. You can then sound out with them the possibility of their becoming your second supervisor, but it is not sensible to ask them directly before talking to your supervisor. This is because there may be reasons that you hadn't known about as to why this may not be such a good idea.

If your supervisor does not make a sensible suggestion for a second supervisor at that next meeting and you cannot suggest a suitable person, then it is probably best to talk to the chair of the postgraduate studies committee and discuss possibilities with them.

If you are in a university that does not appoint second supervisors, then the best thing that you can do is to find one for yourself. In practice, this tends to mean identifying a lab that is good at some technique not used in your main lab that you feel that you want to use and whose PI seems the sort of person you would like as an informal second supervisor. You then have to contact them and ask if you could use their facilities for what they will think is a good reason. In due course, they may become interested in you and your project and you will be able to talk to them about your work. They will then be on the way to becoming an informal second supervisor.

Even better, you and the other graduate students can make a communal complaint about the Department not routinely appointing second supervisors and asking them if they could change the policy.

CHAPTER 11: THE SECOND YEAR OF A PHD – JUST RESEARCH

It may sound odd to say so, but this may be one of the best years in your research career. This is because you should have a clear view of what you want to do, the technical knowledge to do it and no distractions in the way of theses or papers to write, jobs to look for, grants to write or teaching to do. This is really the year when you discover for yourself whether you are good (as opposed to good enough) at research and whether you enjoy it.

Table 11.1 gives you a set of aims for the year. The key one is that you break the back of your PhD work so that your last year can focus on polishing your results, writing the work up as a thesis and papers, deciding on what you want to do next and looking for a position.

Table 11.1: Some aims for the second year

1: Firm up some preliminary research questions. Your research work should start answering them.

2: Sharpen the questions in the light of your results.

3: Keep good records, preferably on your computer. Back up everything in the cloud.

4: Professionalise your skills so that you can collaborate with other people.

5: Maintain your transferable skills (e.g. write a useful computer program).

6: If English is not an easy language for you, attend a course on writing.

7: Attend seminars in your own and other areas

8: Give an internal talk.

9: Keep up with the literature.

10: Do something useful for the departmental postgraduate group.

11: Join your appropriate scientific society, if you haven't done so already.

12: Apply for and attend at least one research meeting. Apply for funds to do this (this will be easier if you have a poster).

13: Do a little teaching of any sort.

14: Be willing to look after an undergraduate honours student in the lab.

Note: Your supervisor will of course be their real

supervisor.

Research questions

Your planning for this year is underpinned by what you will need for your thesis. Most countries will expect it to include at least three strong and linked research chapters and the easiest way to think about each is as answering a question, testing a hypothesis or developing a technique or tool that you will use to help answer the other two questions. Success in answering these questions will mean that writing your thesis and papers will be easier than you might have feared (see Chapter 14).

These chapters do not have to be of equivalent difficulty or sophistication. It is sensible for the first to be what is known as thesis-fodder and may be concerned with defining the properties of your system. Such work is useful, sensible and can be done with little risk (e.g. the expression pattern of a gene in some developing organism, the types of cells present in an in vitro organelle and how they change with time, the restrictions under which some event can take place). The significance of such a chapter is that solid results will come in regularly during your second year and will sustain you while you are also working on more difficult projects.

The second question that you should try to answer should be tougher and more interesting, but it ought to be well-founded and likely to give some interesting results. It will provide the substance of your thesis and will almost certainly be based around the original project that attracted you to in the first place.

At this stage, you can be a little vague about the third question that you will want to follow up in your last research chapter. You may have a clever idea, or something may emerge from the two well-defined questions that is worth following up as a result, say, of looking at the system with a new technique or by modulating standard conditions. With luck, some interesting results will emerge that you can explore. You are not going to focus on this third question now, but you are going to think about it and play a little too. Your scientific instincts should tell you if something interesting and worth following up comes from this work.

If it does, your first step is to clarify what is going on in this area. You will now really be doing your own research and it should give you a real buzz of excitement. Here, you need to keep good notes, even of experiments where nothing special apparently happens: one can never be sure which experiment may, with hindsight, have been important. But note: it is your solid understanding of your system, its properties and even its eccentricities that will help you recognise that something visually or numerically new has happened. Nobel prizes have been won by scientists who first noted that things that should have happened didn't happen and *vice versa*, and then followed up on their anomalous results.

After about six months of work, you should stand back and appraise how things are going, where are the successes and where are the failures, and how you should build on the former and cope with the latter. Once things are clear in your mind, you should write a summary paper. It doesn't have to do much more than give the main lines of research and the key results, perhaps with references back to your notebook. You should then ask your supervisor for a meeting to review where you are with a view to planning the next five months (you are allowed a summer vacation at the end of the academic year!). Things should now go fast and, by the end of your second year, the general shape of your thesis should be clear, and the three questions that will underpin your thesis should be well-formulated and well on the way to being answered.

Hint. *You will be over-busy in year three and time will be saved if your main results from year two, be they tables, images or graphs, are in a state where they can be dropped into your thesis.* Good images with their detailed annotations should be secondarily stored in a *good results* folder together with summary graphs, a document of good ideas for the thesis and anything else of interest. If you don't have any other way of identifying them (e.g. an experiment number), make sure that everything can be traced back to the date on which the experimental work was done.

It is also possible that you are approaching the stage when you can draft your first paper, and you will recognise this because you have asked a new and interesting question and are well on the way to answering it – the main lines of the solution are clear and you are just doing confirmatory work. If you have reached this exciting moment, you should draft a title and abstract and have another meeting with your supervisor to see whether your ideas are well-founded and how to proceed (see Chapter 14). All postgraduates should aim to publish at least one paper that they can bind into their thesis; it will give you confidence and it will add a sheen to your CV.

Other aims

One of the aims in Table 11.1 was to become so good at some techniques that other, perhaps more senior people will ask you to help them out. Provided only that you are not overwhelmed by your own work at that moment and any new work will not be too much of a distraction, such collaborations are always a good idea. They have the advantage of bringing you into the ambit of other groups and their work. Before you do get involved, however, it is good manners to tell your supervisor and also to think about the extent to which to which you should get involved with the work (you can ask graduate students in the other group about the project). With luck, you will get your name on another paper, but the price of doing so should not be getting behind with your own work.

The other aims for the year include moving towards becoming a professional: giving talks at lab meetings (very useful, particularly for getting feedback on tricky problems), presenting papers at journal clubs, maintaining and strengthening your transferable skills and joining your professional society as a student member. This last is particularly important as many such societies have funds that allow postgraduates to attend their meetings. Your application will be strengthened if you have a poster to present and, during your second year, it is enough that you have contributed something to a poster that is predominantly the work of someone else (by your third year, you should be the lead author).

One reason to go to such meetings is that you will get the chance to attend talks by world-ranking scientists and it is good to know what such people can do – they set standards that you should aim to meet. Almost all of them will be working outside your direct area and this is another reason to hear them, and any other speaker who looks as if they may have something interesting to say. As a graduate student, it is too easy to focus on your own small area to the extent that you forget how much is happening in the rest of the world[3].

Teaching and demonstrating in practical classes are other things that are worth doing if opportunities present themselves, provided that it and the necessary preparation do not require more than a few hours a week. You need to learn whether you enjoy working with undergraduate students and looking after them in the lab. Once you do start teaching, you will begin to appreciate an unexpected fact: the teacher learns more than the taught! The business of preparation forces you to get back to the simple basics in areas that you thought you knew well. You may find it surprising to find that you need to think harder and read more to help others understand things that you had thought were obvious to you.

All of these added aspects of your second year will enrich your CV and help make you a more professional scientist.

In a perfect research world ....

By the end of your second year, you will have essentially answered something like your initial questions and reformulated them in the light of your results; the result will be that they have become much sharper and more focused. With luck, you will have the first chapter completed, the second on the way to completion and the third at least well formulated. You may even have enough new material to be thinking about a paper. If you have been fortunate beyond measure, you will have discovered something new and exciting to the extent that the whole focus of your PhD has changed.

You should end the year by reviewing all that you have done and preparing a short paper saying where you are now and what you plan to do in your final year. This paper should be the focus of the end-of-the-year meeting with your supervisor. *Note*: many universities need such a paper before they will allow you to proceed to final-year status. It is required to reassure the postgraduate studies committee that you are serious and on course towards successful completion of your PhD - so you should not write it in such a way as to give the committee cause for doubt. After all this, you will have earned your holiday!

The reality at the end of the year 2

Unfortunately, most people are not at this stage after 24 months of research, although they are well on their way. They will have a fair number of minor results, but they are not quite sure where they are going: the questions may not even be fully formulated, let alone answered. Do not worry! This is quite usual, and the reality is that you will almost certainly be at that ideal state around December. You should still write that summary paper on where you are, and it will be the basis of a where-am-I-going discussion with your supervisor. Now, more than at any other time, you need your supervisor to talk through what you have done and where you should focus. They have a lot more experience than you, and you need to benefit from it.

After all this, you will all need a holiday away from the lab to clear your head. Take it! You will come back refreshed.

CHAPTER 12: THE FINAL YEAR OF A PHD

While the second year may have been one of the best years in your research career, this final year will inevitably be one of the hardest because there is so much that you have to do, if it is to go well. Table 12.1 gives some key aims for the year. In this chapter, we just consider how to finish up your research and to integrate those final experiments within the context of a thesis plan. Writing a thesis, preparing papers for publication and planning a postdoc are sufficiently meaty topics to justify the own chapters.

In principle, you should enter this year with a reasonable body of work behind you that you aim to complete and you should also know pretty well how to do it. Unfortunately, being at this stage is the exception rather than the rule, and most people don't reach it until December, although they have a good idea of what they are doing. If you do not feel that you have even reached this stage, do not despair, but go straight to the Appendix at the end of this chapter; it should give you hope.

Table 12.1: Key aims for the final year
1: Finish your thesis research.
2: Write up your thesis.
3: Write up any papers that derive from your thesis.
4: Give talks and posters.
5: Think about what you want to do next.
6: Get yourself a postdoc or other position.
7: Grow increasingly independent of your supervisor.

A draft thesis plan

Once you have clarified in your mind the key questions that your research will answer, your lab work becomes integrated with how you will write up that work. You therefore need to start formulating how your thesis will be structured far earlier than might expect. Making a draft thesis plan early gives you some insight into what you will be wanting to include in your final thesis (see Chapter 15). The route is always easier if you know, or at least have a good idea of where you are going to end up.

Start by writing down as bullet points, the new results that you have discovered so far; this is the essence of your thesis and will help you organise the introduction (you want to end it by asking questions to which these bullet points are the answer) and structure the experimental chapters. They will also help you work out whether these chapters will be seen as sequential or independent. At this point you can briefly work through the expected organisation of each, starting with the question that it seeks to answer and what the actual answer is or is likely to be.

This basic thesis structure will help you formulate in advance the experiments whose results you will need, while writing it may suggest that you need to repeat experiments that you have already done, partly to give the results more statistical weight and partly to ensure that your data and images are of publishable quality. You need to be honest and critical with yourself here.

Once you have the basic structure of your thesis and the associated work plan, you should make an appointment with your supervisor and send them the two documents. At that meeting, you can ask whether the research programme will be adequate, whether your controls are strong enough (a frequent question at vivas) and whether the thesis structure works well. At this point, you may be a bit surprised at the amount of extra work your supervisor may want you to do.

You should also be aware that there is a natural tension between you and your supervisor. You want your thesis out as soon as possible, while your supervisor, for all that they would like to see you submit and do well, is particularly interested in the papers you can publish together - this is what they need for their grant reports and hence for the good of the lab. You will not want to cross your supervisor, but you should make them aware that your key priority has to be to submit the thesis before you run out of money and need another job. Ideally, you will come to a negotiated settlement on what can realistically be achieved in the time available or they will suggest that they can find a little money to sustain you for an extra three months. This may be a worse choice because PIs taking on postdocs tend to like to run their lab around the academic year.

In the limits, it is your thesis and you have to defend it, not the supervisor. You need to find out what the supervisor thinks is the minimum acceptable amount of extra work for the thesis and what more might be necessary for good publications. You will agree to do the thesis work and, if there is time, try to do the extra work that will be needed for the publications. And you really should try to do it, partly to strengthen your reference and partly because you will need to publish good papers if you are to do well in the future. If you have already decided to do a postdoc in the same area as your PhD, a brief discussion of the labs to which you could apply might be part of this general discussion.

Jonathan Bard

The work of the year

The next thing that you should do is to produce a timetable that covers the timing of both the remaining experimental and other research work and the drafting of your thesis. Plan to do as much as possible as early as possible because the final stages will always take longer than you expect. The easiest parts of the thesis to write are the *Materials and Methods* and the *Introduction*. For the latter you will need to think through how to start with a broad problem in your general area of research and work out how to end with the detailed questions that you will investigate, embedding within this narrative the many papers that you will need to cite (see Chapter 14).

Early in your final year, you should give an internal talk in the lab or to a postgraduate group about your work and what further experimental work you need to do. Feedback at this stage is much better than feedback later when it is too late to incorporate it into your work. You should also go to research meetings and present a poster of your work, both for feedback and for exposure to potential PIs looking for postdocs. A key part of meetings is that they are employment markets.

If you work manically hard in the lab and spend the time when you are tired on the boring but necessary tasks of organising the literature and producing images and graphs, you will probably have your work and thesis draft in fairly good condition some eight months into your final year. For the remaining few months, you will focus on the writing and a few experiments designed to clarify other results, produce better figures for the thesis and finish any statistical analyses that are still incomplete[4]. The aim is always to finish on time with all the base work for your publications completed.

If you are likely to run out of time and money ......

You will realise that this may happen at least three months in advance so you should try to handle things sooner rather than later. You cannot assume that more money will be available, but you should ask your supervisor for additional funding, mentioning that this will allow you to do some extra work from which the lab will benefit. Another possibility is for you or your supervisor to ask the head of your department if they can give you support. Your application will carry more weight if you can give some good reasons as to why you will be late in submitting your thesis, and some examples are given in Table 12.2.

Table 12.2: Good reasons for not finishing a PhD on time

There have been major problems in the lab.
There was a fire.
There was a severe infection in the animal house that held you back.
Your supervisor ran out of money and you had to

change your project.

Something major went wrong and it really wasn't your fault.

Your project was published by someone else in year 3 and you had to change focus.

You have been ill and have medical notes to confirm the time it took to get better.

There have been major domestic crises.

What all these problems have in common is that they were not your fault. *If problems like this arise, the absolute rule is that you tell your supervisor(s) about them immediately and that they (or you) report them to the head of the departmental postgraduate committee as soon as possible.* This is particularly important if you need a formal extension that needs to be authorised by this committee. In practice, it is normally straightforward to get a short-term extension (perhaps 3 months) for minor reasons such as some extra experiments are required, or you need a little more time to write up. Things become trickier if you need more time than this (particularly if you are part of 4-year doctoral training programme) and the delay cannot be blamed on anyone else. The basic rule for extensions is that Postgraduate Studies Committees are far more generous when the reasons for the request clearly reflect events for which there is evidence that it is not your fault. Do not expect sympathy if you cannot provide that evidence.

Try very hard to submit on time

Completing your thesis on time matters for several reasons.

Running out of money is both stressful and debilitating. If there is no money in the department and you have no savings, you may have to depend on parents or a loan or even get a distracting job (working in a bar is one standard way of earning a living that leaves you free to write during the day)

You are far likelier to get a job with a complete than an incomplete thesis. Would you want to take on someone who will spend their first three months of your grant money working on something irrelevant to the needs of your lab?

Completing on schedule not only looks good but sends an implicit message to anyone who reads your CV: it shows that you are a person who knows how to deliver on time.

If, by the time you hand in your thesis, you have already published and/or submitted a paper or two, your CV sends the additional message that you have been unusually efficient as a postgraduate student, and are likely to be so again in any future lab in which you are a postdoc.

All that said, the working rule is that everyone who submits a thesis that is at least reasonable is likely to get their PhD. The worst that usually happens is that you are asked to rewrite some of it or to do a little more work.

Finally, a word on the relationship between you and your supervisor. At the beginning, you were probably quite dependent on your supervisor for academic support. By the beginning of the third year, you should be well on the way to independence, with your supervisor being someone you discuss options with rather than someone who tells you what to do. By the time you submit your thesis, the relationship should have matured further to the extent that you are colleagues, albeit that the supervisor is the senior one.

A key aim of this year is that you learn to take control of your research and become an adult scientist. This is not to say that you have no more to learn, there is always more to learn, but that you should be well on the way to knowing what you want to achieve and having the tools and the confidence to get it. You should be ready to walk out of your lab and be prepared for a new one, while what you have learned from your research, together with the transferable skills you have acquired, will enable you to tackle a host of non-research options. Aim to get this sense of control.

Appendix

If things really have gone badly for you in your second year, and you are starting your final year in a state of despair, perhaps this story will give you hope.

One of my colleagues, whose research was in

area near to one in which I had recently worked, left Edinburgh in September for a job abroad. Before leaving, they asked me if I would take on their research student, who was about to enter her final year and was well on her way. It soon turned out that they had been more than economical with the truth: the student knew the area and had learnt some techniques, but had no results of any use that could be included in a thesis. She then told me that she was determined to finish on time. I took a deep breath and explained to her that she would quickly need to come up with three research questions to answer and that, while they didn't have to be too difficult, they really needed to be answerable. I then suggested that she come back a week later having had some ideas.

She did and she had. We then spent an hour honing these questions and talking about the precise experiments that she should do to answer them. I warned her that it was possible to complete the work and write up in a year, but she would need luck and shouldn't expect any sleep.

That student then started working and I was really impressed by the energy and commitment that she showed. Suddenly things started going well. After six months, I was able to ask the departmental head for some necessary consumable costs to fund the last months of her research work, and I could point out how impressively well she had done. It was the easiest grant application that I have ever had to write, and the money was authorised the following day.

For the last four months of that year that student spent days working and nights writing and submitted her thesis on 30th September, the day her studentship ended. The examiners were happy with the work and never was a PhD more efficiently earned. The reference wrote itself!

CHAPTER 13: WHEN THINGS GO WRONG

Almost everything discussed in this book so far has been about the normal, academic trajectory of a graduate student. The great majority of students who step onto that escalator come off at the other end with their degree and just a few scars to remind them that it had not all been easy.

Occasionally, very occasionally, serious problems will arise that you cannot solve without support beyond that supplied by your supervisor or the lab. Some of these have already been discussed, such as you decide that research is not for you (Chapter 9), you run out of time and money (Chapter 12) or you keep getting negative results (Chapter 5). This chapter considers some other horrors, and one reason for including them is that, once you know about them, you may be able to avoid them.

If you do feel that you are being sucked down

into a whirlpool and are losing control, the first thing to realise is that you are not as alone as you may feel. You are unlikely to be the first student in your department to have had this particular crisis to deal with, and there is always experienced and objective help available from at least someone in a group that includes your main supervisor, your second supervisor (if you have one), the chair of the departmental postgraduate studies committee (CPGSC) and your university's health clinic. You need to remember however that *the sooner you discuss your problem with one of them, the easier it will be to solve.* It should be realised, however, that not all problems end with a satisfactory solution. Nevertheless, failure here is very rare, as everyone wants to see students succeed.

Medical problems

Every student goes through emotional ups and downs during their postgraduate years. If, however, you begin to feel that things are hopeless, you need to go to your health clinic as soon as possible. All universities have doctors who understand student depression and will be able to help you and also check that your depression is not a downstream effect of some disease. People who are ill feel depressed.

If you are diagnosed as having something physically or mentally wrong, you must immediately get a sick note that you can give to your supervisor and department. This is because it is much easier to get a thesis suspension or extension (and perhaps some financial support) for documented medical reasons than for anything else. A suspension is when the thesis clock is officially stopped for, say a period of ill health, and you should ask for it if this is what your doctor suggests. If you are seeing the doctor because your work has been affected for more than a couple of weeks, you need to tell your supervisor so that you can discuss possible courses of action with them.

It should go without saying that you should always follow your doctor's advice.

Problems with your project

What should you do when you are into your last year and everything is going wrong? For example, the system is not behaving as it should, you are getting inconsistent results, and important techniques that should work are not behaving properly (and you have checked that you can get them to work in other contexts). This is a challenge that you should initially try to sort out for yourself, although it is sensible to mention the problems to your supervisor, saying that you are working on what to do and would like to make an appointment in a week's time when you will let them know how things are going and perhaps consider whether it is time for a rethink about this aspect of the project.

You should start by asking yourself the sort

of question that any supervisor would ask you. Is the hypothesis that you are testing or the question you are asking well-founded? Would your negative results be positive in the context of another hypothesis or question? If you are trying to develop a technique, can you break it down into steps and test the component parts? If you can solve the problem yourself by thinking through to an alternative approach that works, you will have come to grips with the sort of problem all research workers eventually face and the ability to have got through such a crisis once will give you confidence for the future. You will have become a better and more resilient scientist.

[margin note: Problem solving.]

But you should not suffer alone for too long. Once you are convinced that things are heading for a dead end (and a week may not be enough), you should go back to your supervisor, explain what you have done to try to solve the impasse and see what they come up with. If the problem that you are working on really is going nowhere, the two of you should be able to come up with a related project that should be more productive. Finally, and before you abandon your original project, see if there is anything that you can salvage from it that can go into your eventual thesis (e.g. one obvious line of research is to ask that question and answer it with "this turns out to be unhelpful because ....").

Another problem that occurs more frequently than one would like is that research funding dries up because a grant application has failed to be funded. Here, the department may feel it is sensible for you to move to another supervisor in a new lab. If you are still in your second year of research, it may be best to move to a new but related project, one close to the interests of your new lab head who will become your first supervisor, with your original supervisor becoming your second – this is really for them to work out.

If you feel that, even though you are near the beginning of your project, you like your system and want to continue working on it with your supervisor, then you need to rethink your research programme and see if there is something interesting that you can do on a much reduced budget (in this case, you will again need to involve the CPGSC as you may have to ask the department for money and hope that they do).

If the crisis occurs when you are into the final year of your original project and things are going well, the solution may be to change lab, but carry on with the same project or one very closely related but perhaps a little nearer to the interests of the new lab. Provided your new lab head is happy, this may be the best thing to do. Indeed, if you have got on well with your original supervisor, you will be doing them a great favour by continuing their work as your results, duly acknowledged, may become the preliminary work for their next grant application. *Hint*: *Always be willing to do favours for others as you never know when you will want them to help you.* Either way, you need to ensure that the CPGSC knows what is going on as being forced to change labs is a good reason for asking for a thesis extension later,

If the reality is that, in your new lab, it is no longer possible to continue with your original or a related project, you now face a substantial scientific problem. This is to work out research questions in a new area that are not only soluble but that you can answer in a reasonable amount of time. A first step is to consider first how much of what you have done meshes with the interests of the new lab and so can be used in your thesis and, second, what technical expertise you have that can be applied to work in the new lab.

Although your new supervisor should be able to provide you with a project, working out for yourself what you want and can do will be very beneficial for your confidence and resilience, and you may even find that you enjoy the challenge. What will have helped here is all the preliminary work that you will have done on your system and the hard-nosed discussions you have had with your original supervisor. You are not the same person who originally walked into the department as a new student.

If you are in this situation, have a conversation with your new supervisor about possible projects and then ask for a week to think about what you might do. Immediately start reading around the subject area and the details of your supervisor's suggestions and then talk to the people in the lab to see what they are working on and the techniques that they are using. After that week, you should be sufficiently up to speed to take a view of what you feel is the aspect of the research that you want to follow and what you want to do. You can then have a good discussion with your new supervisor, who should be impressed by how sophisticated you have become in their area! More important, you are learning to take control of your own work.

But now, you will be behind on your PhD schedule and are going to have to work faster than you might have liked. You may also need technical help and you will find that, if you are polite, enthusiastic and competent, people can be very generous. You have been put in an unreasonable situation, but, by making the most of the change to a new lab, you will have grown as a scientist.

Problems with your supervisor

One problem that can arise is that you feel that your project is not your own, that you are being treated as your supervisor's technician and that you are being given no freedom. Your supervisor's response may be along the lines of "I am trying to ensure that your research goes well and fast, and that we can publish papers so that you will get a good PhD". Your supervisor is deliberately missing the points that making mistakes is one key part of graduate education and that ownership of your project is another. If, when you raise this with your supervisor, you get nowhere, you will need to discuss this with the CPGSC and, if your supervisor eventually says that they don't have another project and you should accept what is on offer, you may need to change supervisors (and this is much easier if you have a second supervisor with whom you are on good terms). Usually, however, supervisors will be prepared to step back and suggest that you do some of their work, but start on a related project that will be your own.

Occasionally, a supervisor will leave for another job and, even if there is an offer to accompany them, you don't want to go. There are several good reasons for this: you may have domestic reasons for not moving, you may not want to waste the six months that it will take before the new lab is up and running or there might be visa problems. It is the job of the department to sort this out and is yet another reason why having a second supervisor is so useful. If you do not have a second supervisor, it will be best if you can think of a lab that you would want to move to and to think carefully about what you can bring to that lab in the way of technical expertise. ***Hint***: *Whenever you want something from someone, it is important for you to put yourself in their place and ask yourself what is in it for them if they say yes, and to consider what you need to do to get them to say yes.*

Very, very occasionally, relationships between you and your supervisor break down completely. You need to tread carefully here because the department will instinctively side with your supervisor, particularly if they have a good track record with students. In this case, you will need to talk to the CPGSC, and you will not want them to think that it is you who is being difficult. What will help if this happens is that, irrespective of the details of the breakdown in the relationship, you will have kept a log of occasions when things have gone wrong with a summary of what happened. It will however always be better if you have an informal chat with the CPGSC before things get too bad and they help sort things out. You don't want to change your supervisor if you can possible avoid it. Not only will this slow the progress of your research work, but you risk poisoning your relationship with your original supervisor.

The worst thing that can happen is that your supervisor turns out to be useless in providing support and help. It is rare that they are incompetent, but they can either lose interest in students or have no time for them because other commitments are far more immediate. If you cannot make appointments with your supervisor or if you cannot get their attention when you need it, your thesis and career is at risk. If this happens, you are unlikely to be the only one suffering. You will need to complain to the CPGSC, and these complaints carry much more weight if they come from all the graduate students in the lab. You should know if all of you are having a hard time, or whether it is you alone. If the former, the supervisor clearly cannot then argue that it is your fault or that you keep bothering them with trivia.

If there are problems of this nature, it is important that you and your fellow students keep a diary of failed meetings. In practice, no academic wants to get a reputation as a bad supervisor and an initial expression of concern or a quiet word from the CPGSC may well be all that is needed to bring your supervisor back on track. You also need to remember that supervisors are human and can have personal problems that may affect their professional competence (see Chapter 10). This is not something that you can solve, but it might be something that you could mention to the CPGSC.

Problems with other people in lab

Although most research labs are fairly informal environments, you should never forget that they are places of work and the normal courtesies apply. If someone senior asks you to do something, you should do it. If someone needs help, you should try to provide it. If there are communal jobs to be done, you should do your fair share. If people are seen to be difficult in the lab, life for them can become isolated and uncomfortable. So, if misunderstandings or problems arise, sort them out as soon as possible; apologise if it you are at fault and everyone can move on. You need to be a good citizen in the lab and, if you are not, everyone will soon know it, especially your supervisor, even if they are rarely there.

One problem that sometimes arises is personal relationships that go wrong. Labs are full of unattached people and relationships form naturally and easily. When they are going well, it is a pleasure (although the two of you need to remember that there are others in the lab too and it is not a place for private behaviour). Problems can, however, arise when things are going badly and particularly when one side wants to end the relationship leaving the other stressed and unhappy. If this happens, you must be as professional as possible in the lab and ensure that others don't suffer because one of you is having a hard time. Neither of you wants to have to leave the lab for the sake of their mental well-being, but this may be the only solution if you cannot keep your emotions under control during the working day. With luck, however, your research work will keep you sane until the emotional stresses blow over.

A particularly serious problems arises when someone, particularly a senior person, starts to behave in a sexually inappropriate way or makes you feel that you are being bullied. In the first instance, warn them off and make a dated note of what happened on your computer. If the behaviour continues to happen, complain to your supervisor or to the chair of the PGSC committee. This complaint will carry much more weight if you can provide diary notes. The first complaint can be very informal, but the second has to go to the chair of the PGSC, the head of department or a harassment officer, should the department have one – people have no right to hassle you.

Crises outside of the lab

Obvious examples are problems in your domestic arrangements (e.g. your landlord wants to throw you out of your flat), your help is needed at home because there are family health problems or a bereavement, you have a financial crisis, or your marriage or partnership breaks down. Your supervisor and department may not be able to help solve these problems directly, but they may be able to provide some support. If you have to go home for a while, for example, others in the lab may be able to complete experiments that are running (yet another reason for keeping on very good terms with the rest of the lab!). If you let your supervisor and the CPGSC know what is happening, they may allow you extra time at the end of your studentship to complete (although a couple of weeks of crisis is probably not enough for an extension).

Crises and bad luck can happen to anyone and their solution depends on having several means of support. Key here are your main supervisor, a second supervisor (if you have one) and a good PGS committee with a sympathetic chair, together worth other members of the lab. What will also be important is support from friends outside the department – you do sometimes need to forget academe. It may also help if you are in a department that has a little uncommitted money that is available to help sort out student crises. Most students will go through their postgraduate years able to handle the problems that come their way, but it helps to have your support network in place just in case the gods frown on you.

CHAPTER 14: WRITING YOUR FIRST PAPER

If things have gone well, you may be ready to publish a paper or two. This chapter discusses when your research is at a stage to do this[5] and how to write it up for the scientific public. It deliberately comes before the chapter on writing PhD theses to encourage you to write your first paper before you submit your thesis.

If you think you may be ready to write a paper for publication, you should first ask yourself the following test questions:

- Have I asked a substantial question and got a substantial answer?
- Have I tested an interesting hypothesis and either confirmed or disproved it?
- Have I developed a useful technique and shown that it works better than alternatives or does something that they cannot?

How to Become a Scientist

> Have I made a new and interesting observation that I have followed up sufficiently to provide a convincing explanation?
>
> Are my results robust, properly controlled and supported by the appropriate statistical analyses

If the answer to any of these questions is "yes" you are through to the second stage. To get further, you need to be able to convince others that you have passed the quality-control threshold in that the work is useful or interesting or substantial. If you are still convinced that your work is worth publishing, you also need to be sure that the work makes a complete narrative. Note that these criteria are absolute: honours and MSc projects can be worth publishing - the academic level of the author is irrelevant.

First steps

First, write down your key new observations and results as bullet points in as simple a way as possible together with the question to which they provide the answer; you may also need to include some key data (e.g. a table, graph or image). If this work, simply expressed, does not convince you that you have enough to answer that questions you will need to do more work. Do not however be over-critical at this stage or you will never publish anything.

Next, produce a title, which includes the key point that you will want people to remember in as few words as possible. Then, draft an abstract which includes the question and why it matters, how you went about answering it, the key results and their significance, all in not more than about 200 words. Leave this text for a day or two and then polish it, the title and the bullet points. You are now ready to see your supervisor and get their view, so let the supervisor know what you have done giving them your single page of text and any associated key data and make an appointment to see them as soon as possible.

Your supervisor should be delighted with what you have done as you have shown initiative and they may well get a publication to add to their own CV. While they should be enthusiastic, remember that it is their job to be critical and to give you a hard time about the adequacy of the work. The net result of the meeting will probably be that there is something good in what you have done, but it may need a little more work. A more difficult answer is "yes, the work is worth publishing but you would get it published in a much better journal, one with a higher impact factor, if you did considerably more work". Your supervisor might feel, for examples, that the new technique should be used to get some interesting data or that the question you have answered have led directly to another question and it would be better to publish answers to both. You will also at this stage consider whether anyone else in the lab has made a contribution to the work that justifies co-authorship.

Your response might be that you want to carry on in research and, although the work could be strengthened, it would be better to get something out now for the strength of your CV. I do however have to say that the literature is full of small papers that got lost and your supervisor might be right. A compromise might be to present your work as a talk or poster at a scientific meeting for which the abstracts are published in a journal. This establishes your ownership of the work as a preliminary study that can later be followed up with a full paper. This paper will refer back to the published abstract, perhaps in a footnote

The writing process

On the assumption that your supervisor says that the work is worth publishing perhaps with slightly better data, you will leave their office with a spring in your step. It won't last long however as writing papers is a slow and difficult business. The important thing at this stage is to set those remaining experiments in motion and start drafting. As you know roughly what you will want to say, it makes some sense to write an outline of the paper that gives the sections and subsections together with the captions of the figures you will include. You can then write a rough and quick first draft, starting with the introduction and ending with the discussion. That done, you can improve sections in any order. One of the benefits of writing papers is that the logic of the scientific argument can suggest further experiments that clarify or extend the work; you will need to get going on these.

At this stage, the work can go into your CV under the heading "*Paper in preparation*". Although this does not carry a lot of weight, it does signify that you are at least on the way to completing a substantial piece of work and are prepared to talk about it.

The standards for writing a scientific paper are higher than those for a thesis because editors like terse rather than easily readable prose. You will have to polish and shorten your text in successive drafts, while still trying to make the text easy to read. *Hint: One test here is to read your prose out loud and listen to how it sounds. If, as you listen to the text, it doesn't flow naturally and logically, you need to do improve it.*

Fortunately, you are not writing the paper on your own, but with your supervisor and, in due course, with any secondary authors. If the list is not obvious, the rule is that authorship requires that, were things to go wrong with some part of the results, that person would be prepared to take public responsibility. If you and your supervisor decide that the paper requires a contribution from a further author or two, you should contact them to let them know early that a paper that will need to include their work is being drafted, and ask them if they are happy with this and, if so, to draft some text and figures.

The task of writing is not quite as bad as it is might seem if you start off with a good first draft. Indeed, once the process is under way and there is a real sense of momentum, drafts and revisions can proceed rapidly. The key thing is that *you control the writing process*. You produce and then edit drafts, you speak to the other authors about which components of their work will be included and ask them to produce figures showing their data, and you decide when to give text to your supervisor to read and comment on (not too much at a time if you want a quick turnaround). Writing a paper and taking ownership of it is one of the most important steps you can take in becoming a professional scientist and you should start as soon as you have something worth publishing. If you can do it before submitting your thesis, so much the better.

Once your supervisor feels that the paper is in a good state, you need to show the text to the secondary authors, incorporate their comments and agree on the order of the names. This can sometimes be contentious. Unless you are in a field where the convention is that authors are listed alphabetically[6], it is normal for the author who did the key part of the work and who should have led the writing of the manuscript, to comes first and the head of the lab (or the supervisor) last, with other people ranked either alphabetically or in order of the strength of their contribution. You will naturally want to be the first author, and you will have guaranteed this by taking responsibility for the writing.

If the paper is mainly the result of equal amounts of work by you and, say, a postdoc, it would be normal for the postdoc to come first and you second (they need first authorship more than you do) but to include a footnote saying that the first two authors shared equally in the majority of the work. It may be wise to leave this ordering, together with that of any other authors, to your supervisor.

Submission

You want your paper to be published in a high-impact and important journal but the standards for getting into these are very high. The decision on where to publish should probably be left to your supervisor, particularly if it is a journal which charges for submission. It may turn out to be best to send a paper to a specialist journal in your field, partly to ensure that people who know about the area get to see it, but also because the editor will be someone who knows about the field. The really high-impact journals such as *Nature* have professional editors and your paper may be handled by someone who knows very little about your specific area of research.

Here, it can be a good idea to let your supervisor handle discussions with the journal, particularly if you are under time pressure, even if this means that your supervisor becomes the corresponding author (you will still be the first author). In your final year, you will probably have other and more important things to do. You will still learn quite a lot by being part of the publication process, as you will both have to deal with the comments of reviewers and the editor.

Once that paper is submitted, it gets added to your CV as "*Paper under review*", and you will wait for the response from the journal. This is very rarely as kindly as you may hope as it is the job of reviewers to be critical. They may ask you to polish the prose, shorten the text and even to do some more work and you will not be pleased. Your response to the reviewers' comments should be comprehensive, answering each point with what you intend to do about it. Normally, you will accept the comments, but, should you feel that the reviewers have got something wrong, give your reasons for not following their suggestions. Even if the reviewers are brutal and reject your paper, check their comments carefully (before doing this, I normally allow a couple of days to get over being rejected). Reviewers can be wrong and, if you and your supervisor think they are, make your points to the editor who may well send the paper to another referee for an independent view. This is more likely to happen for a specialist than a more general journal because the editor will understand your arguments (see above).

Once the negotiations with the editor have

finished, you should know exactly what you need to do to get the paper finally accepted. You should do the necessary experimental work, revise the text and resubmit the paper as soon as possible. Eventually and with a little luck you will have met all the complaints and criticisms that the reviewers have thrown at you and your paper will have been accepted for publication. One advantage of having had to deal with reviewers' comments at this stage is that your work will have passed a high standard of criticism before your thesis examiners get to see it.

Your then promote the paper in your CV to "*in press*". This stage should not last long and, as soon as the paper is available on line, you have a proper paper for your CV, one that you can bind into your thesis.

If you have publishable results, you should publish them

If, after your PhD, you decide to leave academe, you may feel that you have no interest in publishing your work and that, if it matters to your supervisor, they can do it. This is entirely the wrong approach, if only because you risk your supervisor saying in their reference for you that, for all your virtues, you are someone who finds it hard to complete work that you have started. It is far better to realise that publishing your work is part of the training that you get from doing a PhD. Moreover, you will feel proud seeing your name in print.

One final point: it is important to write up your research as soon as you have something substantial to say. If you don't, you take the risk that your interests will change, and that you have neither the time nor the mental energy to write those papers. The net result is that all this research will remain forgotten, lurking at the far edge of your computer's hard drive. It is still on my conscience that I have the drafts of three papers that have not and never will be submitted for publication. Life moved on and all that research effort was wasted.

CHAPTER 15: WRITING UP A PHD THESIS

You have done the basic work for three research chapters, each of which asks and answers a question or the like, you have a pile of methods, you know a fair amount of the background to your research work and have a set of references neatly formatted. How do you begin to put all this together into a thesis?

The easiest but toughest model of a PhD thesis is the set of your publications that is introduced by a review of your subject; this sort of thesis is often published as a small book. It is the easiest format to produce as all the hard work of writing has been done in advance, but it does take a long time to produce those papers. Most universities will let you submit your thesis in this format, if you have been productive enough to have published three or four solid papers.

The most common style is that you write up your work in a thesis and bind into it any papers that you have published. As this thesis will only be read by you, your supervisors and your examiners, you will want it to be in as useful a format as possible. The best way to do this is to write each of your experimental chapters as a distinct research paper. Each chapter asks a single question and has its own detailed introduction discussing the background to this question, together with sections for specialised methods, research work and a discussion which focuses on establishing the answer to the question. These three or perhaps four research chapters will be prefaced by a general introduction that leads up to the questions that the thesis asks, and is immediately followed by a chapter of general materials and methods. The thesis concludes with a general discussion which starts with the conclusions you have reached in the research chapters, goes on to considers the significance of these answers in the wider context of the field and ends with future lines of research.

This format makes it straightforward to produce the research papers that you will submit for publication in journals as you will already have done all the hard work of writing. All you will need to do is to polish and shorten the texts of the experimental chapters and remove some of the experimental detail that is expected in a thesis, but taken for granted in a research publication, which is expected to be terse. If things have gone really well, your thesis will result in three papers and perhaps a review from your introduction, all of which can be produced in a month or so.

Remember: writing your thesis will take longer than you expect (what doesn't?), so start working on it early. The writing alone will probably take three or four very full months. Given that you will almost certainly need to do some experimental work at the same time, it is sensible to start thinking about your thesis and drafting its structure as soon as possible in your final year, and writing preliminary text at least six months before you hope to submit it.

How to get started
Your department will set progress hurdles for you to jump over before you are allowed to get to the thesis-writing stage. If this is a thesis summary, it will probably include a draft title and abstract, a brief introduction, summaries of your research results together with what research you still need to do, and thoughts about your conclusions. If so, draft the document and show it to your supervisor so that you can incorporate their comments before submitting it. One question to ask them is whether secondary or apparently irrelevant material should be included. You should do this as early as possible so as to receive useful feedback, although your supervisor may also suggest some necessary further work that you hadn't thought about.

Once the summary has been approved, you need to make a skeleton outline of your thesis. This is a set of topic headings that usually include **chapter titles**, *major headings* and *subheadings* together with *minor headings* which can be used at the beginning of paragraphs (note that the levels should be distinguished by font type). You may want to number them as this is helpful in keeping tabs on where exactly you are within the structure: thus, a minor heading could, for example, be *4.3.3.1 The expression of some gene in the early mouse diencephalon*.

Although this skeleton outline will probably need minor revisions as you write, producing something detailed early on is the key to giving you a sense of momentum. This is because, once you have produced that skeleton, you will have cracked the structure of the thesis. Writing always goes more easily if you have a sense of the direction of the narrative.

The writing habit

Postgraduates do not expect to enjoy writing their thesis. Indeed, many approach it with a sense of trepidation as they have never had to write anything that long; even the thought of it can seem overwhelming. The truth is that, once you get into thesis-writing, things are not as bad as you will have expected. The best insight I have come across about how to write came from a novelist who said: "I can only write when I am inspired, and

I make sure that I am inspired every morning at 9.15". What this means, of course, is that writing requires ritual and discipline.

You will have to work out what rituals suit you, but something like this works for me. I try to sit down at my computer as early as possible in the morning and start work by reading through what I wrote yesterday and polishing it. This puts me in the mood to continue writing and I will try to complete a section or two by lunchtime, and then take a long break. For me, writing, which I have always found a hard and unnatural activity, is easiest when I am fresh. For a graduate student, the writing has to be fitted in with lab work and it may be best if you can schedule that for the afternoon. If you have any strength left, you should work on images and figures in the evening and on weekends (don't expect much of a life while you are writing your thesis).

Hint: *While you are at your computer, keep a notepad beside you to jot down any idea that occurs to you that is not part of the next paragraph.* Once you are buried in your thesis writing, you will get all sorts of odd thoughts and some of them will be useful for other chapters.

The hardest thing to do is to write the first draft; polishing text critically is easier, so start by assembling your ideas, outline and data for each chapter and write a rough draft of the *Material and Methods* to get you going. Then leave it for a day. You will come back to it slightly shocked at how poorly written it is, but you will have something substantial to work on[7]. Then do the same with each *Experimental Chapter*, then the *Discussion* and finally the *Introduction*.

At this stage, you should have a very good idea of the gaps in the scientific logic and know how much more experimental work is needed. While you are doing this, you can start to polish those rough drafts.

Should you feel that you are suffering from *writer's block* and that you cannot cope even with idea of writing, take an immediate break from it. Move to something else which is less stressful, such as producing images and tables with their captions and formatting your references. Slowly move back to writing something that is relatively effortless such as methods, or short such as the abstract.

One of the advantages of having produced a detailed thesis plan is that you will have a wide range of topics in each chapter that can be written independently. The resulting prose can be slotted into the appropriate chapter at the right place. If you do the easy bits at a reasonable pace, you may well find that you acquire the necessary momentum to tackle the harder sections. As mentioned above, the key thing is to distinguish between writing a rough draft of the text and polishing it. Most people find that writing something rough is not too hard and that the later polishing is not as bad as they had expected. You need to end by being perfectionist, but you must not start out being too critical.

The detailed structure

Title and abstract. All scientific writing starts with these and you will know that you are ready to write your thesis when the title becomes obvious and you are ready to write the abstract. This should be 200-250 words that cover the topic and why it matters, the key questions, the basics of the methodology, the major results, the answers to the questions and their significance. This is also the outline of the full narrative of the thesis. Abstract drafts go through several revisions as the thesis proceeds.

Acknowledgements. Be generous and honest as you do not want to take the risk of being accused of plagiarism. Your readers will rightly assume that any work not explicitly mentioned as having been done by someone else has been done by you.

General introduction. Although this comes early in the thesis, you may not want to complete it until after the research chapters have been at least drafted. Remember that the primary purpose of this is not to review the literature, but to introduce what you want to do and why within the context of the literature on your system.

You should start by showing that you have a sense of the historical context of the problems you are working on. You do not need to write a book on the whole field, but should concentrate on the area within which your research sits. The aim is to have a trajectory of thinking that ends up with the exact problems that you aim to solve. Producing this sense of a trajectory in the mind of the reader is not easy as there is so much material that you could include. One way of approaching this problem is to type onto your computer any topic that you could include in the introduction and then try to sort them all into an ordered structure.

Note that you only have to include enough material here to formulate the questions you will ask. The detailed literature around these questions will be included in the introductory section of each experimental chapter.

Aims. Next. you should articulate the questions and hypotheses that your research answers or tests. This will come at the end of the introduction and before the material and methods.

Materials and methods. You will need to decide which of the materials and methods are common to all the work and which are specific to particular research chapters. Here, you may want to include some experimental work demonstrating that the techniques work although it may be enough to include full controls in the research chapters. Because the section on materials and methods is the most straightforward part of the writing, many people write these up first.

Research chapters. These are, of course, the core of the thesis and the ones that will really determine whether you will get a PhD. They should be fairly straightforward to write because you will have read a lot of papers in your field that cover similar questions, so the style should be obvious. Each chapter should focus on one of the questions or aims, and the first part of its introductory section should show that question or aim arises from the known properties of the system (i.e. the associated literature or your earlier chapters). The latter part of the introduction should focus on the research plan and the sequential logic of the work. There should then be a section on the materials and methods that are specific to this chapter which is in turn followed by a lengthy section of results. The purpose of the discussion here is essentially to establish that your results provide the answer to the question you formulated in the introduction, but you will also need to consider their validity and any possible problems with them. The significance of the answer will be covered in the general discussion at the end of the thesis.

The first thing that you should do when thinking about these research chapters is to write down the question and a set of bullet points, each of which reflects something new that you have done, and which together answer the question. If you cannot do this, you may need to do more work and may want to discuss this with your supervisor. Here, you should be your own harshest critic.

If you have already published some or all of the work, you will still need to write up the research, with the focus on what you rather than your colleagues have done. You can still bind a reprint into the thesis as an appendix and add a footnote saying that some of this work has already been published and will be found in that appendix.

Final discussion. Once the experimental chapters have been drafted, your head will probably be so full of information that is should not be too difficult to write a discussion that will start with the conclusions that you have already established. Then show how they illuminate the main topic of the thesis. Finally, describe their wider significance for the area in which you have been working and where they lead in terms of future work.

Writing

You may find it helpful to break your prose down into paragraph-sized thoughts whereby one paragraph makes a specific point that picks up from where the previous one stopped and leads into the next one. After you have written a few paragraphs and there is a natural break, read through those paragraphs and check that the sentences are not too long. If they are, break them down into shorter ones. You should also be careful about using adverbs: their use sometimes means that you have been imprecise and so need to modify what you have written. Some rules for scientific writing are given in Table 15.1.

Table 15.1: Rules on writing scientific prose

1: Be concise but provide enough detail for the text to be easily readable.

2: Exclude all waffle and padding.

3: You can include failures and blind alleys if they exclude options that a reader might consider reasonable (you did!).

4: Ensure that any diagrams or graphs show exactly what you claim.

5: Do not invent imaginary trends or over-interpret your data.

6: Justify your conclusions on the basis of your evidence.

7: In the discussion, separate demonstrated truths from thoughts and speculations.

Thesis mechanics

Here are some useful guidelines as to how to organise your writing.

> Before you start writing, read through the regulations on how your university expects theses to be presented. You really don't want to be told later by the administration that your thesis is in the wrong format and you will need to resubmit it in the proper one.

Once you have produced the outline, open a folder for each chapter and copy all of the material relevant to that chapter into it. Include a file for notes and thoughts (MS notes is useful here). If you have any physical as opposed to digital material, get hold of a box file for each chapter and use it to store that material.

Open separate folders for successive drafts and label each chapter with the draft number (e.g. Material-and-methods-3.doc)

Make a specific folder for all the references. Ensure you know the correct format and set up a template in endnote or the like.

Decide on the style and font that you will use.

Most important of all: make sure that everything on your computer is backed up, both in the cloud and on a memory stick. If your laptop is stolen, you can expect sympathy but no concessions.

Start writing as early as is practical in your final year and expect problems. It is usual, once you get into the writing, that you will realise that some of your data is not good enough or the results of just one more experiment will strengthen your argument. Expect this to happen and allow time to do that experiment.

Graphs, tables and images

These data are the core of your thesis and will be

the major focus of your PhD exam. They have to look good and they have to be sufficiently solid that they raise no concerns with the examiners. There will always be more data that you want to show so choose what you include carefully.

Make sure that all statistical analyses are completed before you start to produce final figures.

If you include tables of data, make sure you include all appropriate significance tests. You may want to use bold font or a colour to highlight important numbers,

Histograms and graphs should be clear. They should also include error bars as appropriate.

Always show controls.

Select your best images and make sure that they are properly annotated with arrows to direct the reader's eye to what you want them to see and magnification bars if needed (magnifications in the caption are a worse and less clear option). If you choose to highlight visual features with Photoshop manipulation, mention this in the caption.

Legends should be clear and free-standing.

Producing images, histograms and graphs of publishable quality takes time. It is always better to have at least drafted reasonable quality figures as soon as you have obtained data. You never want to have to produce beautiful final figures from your raw data at the last minute.

Showing drafts to your supervisor

Having agreed a basic structure for the thesis, you should show early drafts to your supervisor, one chapter at a time. To ask them to do more is to risk their not having time to comment fully. Treat your supervisor as a resource and manage it carefully! This is part of taking control of your thesis – it is your responsibility. You do not have to take your supervisor's advice on any particular point, but, if you don't, you should have a good reason for disagreeing with it.

An important rule here is that, before you hand in a chapter to your supervisor, you should read through your prose carefully, polish it, check the spelling, ensure that the grammar is correct and arrange the text so that the formatting looks neat. **Hint**: *Never, never hand in scruffy text to your supervisor or anyone else; it creates a bad impression.* It is the job of the supervisor to look at the science and the structure of your thesis, not to copy-edit it.

The final thesis

The "book" should look good, read easily and make you feel proud. Your aim is that, when your examiners pick it up and glance through it, the thought that should run through their head is that *the thesis looks good with nothing obviously wrong,* and reading it will not be too daunting (Table 15.2 is a check list of things that set alarm bells ringing in the minds of examiners, so you should always have them in mind as you produce text and figures). There is a psychological point here: if people start reading something in a good frame of mind, they will be sympathetic to it. If, however, they start to think that something may not be right, they will become suspicious of everything, even when they shouldn't be. Do your best to keep the examiners on your side! We will consider all this in a little more detail when we consider PhD oral exams in Chapter 16.

Table 15.2: What worries a thesis examiner?

1: Lack of a narrative and a poor structure.
2: No clear questions asked and answered.
3: No problems posed and solved.
4: Inadequate *Material and Methods* together with inadequate controls.
5: Thin discussion with no "future work".
6: Scruffy-looking pages.
7: Badly written prose.
8: Grammatical and typing errors.
9: References missing or incorrectly cited.
10: Amateur-looking diagrams, graphs and images.
The key points are not clear and magnifications look wrong.
11: Unconvincing statistics
The confidence limits, for example, don't seem to mesh with the data.

CHAPTER 16: PHD EXAMS

The details of the regulations for examining PhD these vary across universities, but they always include written reports and oral exams; they may also require the candidate to give a public talk. Once you have written your thesis in accordance with the detailed format requirements of the university, read through it, read it again, polished it, perhaps shown final drafts to others (sympathetic partners who are in academe are particularly helpful here) and polished it yet again, there is no more that you can do about what will be in those written reports which are submitted before the oral exam.

As to the public presentation, you should already not only have given a seminar on your work and asked for and received feedback, but have the experience of giving regular seminar presentations over the last few years. Public speaking should be one of your skills and this will go well provided that you include clear introductory material, ensure that your slides look good and stick to the structure of the thesis.

The hard part is the oral exam and you will inevitably be nervous because you have no idea what the examiners will throw at you, or even what they are looking for (some ideas on this are given in Table 16.1). If it is any reassurance before you start preparing yourself, you should remember that you are the world expert on your thesis topic because you have been living with it for three years or so; the examiners are coming to the details of your work for the first time. This knowledge, combined with the fact that your supervisor has approved the work, should give you confidence, but should not make you over-confident: one can never predict what will be going on in an examiner's mind.

Table 16.1: what examiners look for in an oral exam

1: You understand your work and its implications.

2: Confirmation that this work is of publishable quality.

3: You have the appropriate background knowledge for the thesis.

4: You have a broad knowledge of the area and the technical literature.

5: You have the appropriate technical and statistical skills.

6: You can discuss and defend your work convincingly with professionals.

Preparation for the oral exam

What you should realise is that the examiners are essentially on your side as no one wants to fail someone at a viva[8]. What the examiners are looking for is summarised in Table 16.1, so your preparation should be aimed at making it easy for you to pass these tests. Things that irritate examiners, a risk you shouldn't take, are given in Table 16.2. What you need to do is sufficient preparation to make you feel reasonably confident on the day. Here are some topics that you should prepare.

The recent literature. It impresses examiners if you can discuss recently published work compatible with what you have done or that is based on your conclusions. Even if another paper disagrees with yours, you can think through why that was and use the information.

Work not included in the thesis. You should think about any work that you have done that is not in the thesis but may be worth mentioning in the oral.

The key literature. Examiners often start a viva by testing you on the literature, particularly key historical papers. Make sure you know about the foundations of your area and your system.

Your system. Examiners often ask apparently simple questions about your area, and your answer should show that you know more about the field than just the technical details of your aspect. Two examples illustrate this. First, a student working in molecular genetics in my department passed the research component of their oral, but the examiners insisted on a second oral three months later focusing on mouse genetics because the candidate's knowledge of this had been woeful. Second, I asked a student working on the molecular basis of gut development some simple questions on gut anatomy. My aim had been to put them at ease, but it turned out that the student knew nothing about the parts of the gut. It was not a good start to an oral exam.

Prepare answers to some obvious questions.

1: What do you think is the most important contribution that this thesis makes?
2: Are your controls robust and are your statistical analyses correct?
3: Can you suggest follow-up experiments to the work in each chapter?
4: Are there other, possibly better techniques that you could have used?
5: What do your results mean for other related areas?

Do your homework on the examiners: Check their interests and recent papers as this may guide their questioning. If one, for example, is an expert in a particular technique you have used, make sure that you know its strengths, limitations and theoretical basis.

There are two other points relevant to oral exams

If there have been crises during your studentship that have not been your responsibility (*e.g.* your supervisor left and you moved to another one, the lab burnt down, or there have been severe family problems), it is the responsibility of your supervisor to let the examiners know. They will not make any allowances for shoddy work, but may be a little more tolerant on the quantity of work, particularly if you perform well in the oral exam.

Finally, many universities allow the supervisor to sit in on the oral exam, but not to make comments, with the choice being left to the student and the supervisor. There are reasons for asking the supervisor to be there: if there is a serious argument, they may help bring it to an end, they can give you confidence, they can witness any difficulties that you may need to mention in an appeal. These are not, in my view, very good reasons. People hoping to be awarded a PhD should be able to look after themselves in an oral exam, and having the supervisor there is an indication of insecurity that the examiners will certainly note. For this reason, supervisors may decline your request, but you should discuss the possibility if you feel that their presence may make things go better.

The oral exam

You will be introduced to the examiners and, if you do not know them, remember their names. If you have any doubts about this, perhaps because you are nervous, note their names and positions on a pad of paper, ideally one that you can pull pages from[9]. They will rapidly move to their first question which will normally be about the academic context of your work (i.e. the literature) and the system. They will then ask you about your research work. In the UK, it is standard to work through the thesis page by page, so you will already have controlled the order of the questioning.

Always answer each question in as precise a way as possible, but you can, if you have any doubts, spend a second thinking about how to want to reply and the last thing you want to say before you stop. Examiners do not like interminable and rambling answers. You may find that your answer stimulates another question on that topic and you are drawn into an argument. If you are sure of your ground, stand up for yourself, but always be polite. You should never say that the examiners are wrong, you should rather say "That is interesting, but ...." or "I understand that argument, but there is counterevidence ....". This is where some of pre-oral work may be helpful.

Table 16.2: What irritates examiners in oral exams

1: You are not enthusiastic and interested.
   If you aren't, why should they be?
2: You cannot defend the design of your work and the interpretation.
3: You cannot explain your statistical analysis.
4: You give rambling replies to questions and reach no

clear conclusions.
5: You can't explain the context of the work adequately.
6: You are not up to date on the literature.
7: You cannot point to some originality in your thesis.
8: You cannot point to some key and novel conclusions.
9: They know more than you on the basics of the project.

One of the subtexts of your oral exam is you! Examiners are happy to award a PhD, but they do like to have some confidence in the person they are awarding it to. This confidence comes mainly from the quality of your work and the sharpness of your answers. It helps just a little if you look like a postdoc rather than a scruffy postgraduate student. So, dress in a way that respects the seriousness of the occasion and that also makes you feel confident and comfortable – you do want to make it easy for them to award you your degree. The last thing that you want to do is to irritate your examiners; Table 16.2 should help you avoid doing this.

Finally, what should you do if they find something wrong in the thesis? The first rule here is also the first rule of politics: *if you are in a hole, stop digging*. Never defend the indefensible. Your aim here is to acknowledge the fault as soon as possible (you can be seen to make a note of it on your pad), and try to move things on as fast as possible to something else that is solid. You should therefore agree that this aspect of the work needs to be corrected, making sure that you understand precisely what is wrong (and you can later ask if all that is required is a better analysis or improved text – you don't want to have to go back to the lab to do more work). One way of acknowledging fault is to say: "Oh dear, did I write that?" implying that it was just careless writing, but you have to be prepared for the follow-up question "What did you mean to say?"

Finally, things will come to an end, you will be thanked and told to go and have a cup of coffee and the examiners will discuss your performance. Do not forget to pick up your notepad before you leave!

After the oral

You may be invited back to the examination room to be given your results or the chair may come and talk to you alone. You of course hope that they will congratulate on a perfect thesis and defence, tell you to publish your remaining research papers and wish you well for your future. This does happen, but not very often. The usual result is that you are told that you have been awarded your PhD, but subject to some corrections to the thesis.

You may think that they have been unfair. This may be so, but you have no choice but to accept their judgement and do the corrections as rapidly as possible. What makes this easier is being given a precise list of what is wrong and what they expect you to do (being told that "the examiners were not happy with the experiment on page 77" is not helpful). It is usual for one of the examiners to take responsibility for checking the corrections and you need to get a detailed list from them of what is wanted. Work hard and rapidly to get those corrections done so that you can resubmit the corrected thesis as soon as possible.

If the examiners are sufficiently unhappy with your thesis and oral, they may be unwilling to grant you a PhD on even an amended thesis, but may offer you a lesser degree such as an MPhil or an MSc if you revise the thesis. The discussion with the committee or its chair now becomes serious. You will be shocked, but need to pull yourself together quickly and ask why, and what would it take for a rewritten thesis to be acceptable for a PhD. Once you are alone, you should immediately make a note of how you think that the oral exam went and then discuss the matter with your supervisor. You need to know if they informed the examiners about any problems and whether they think that the examiners have been unfair. There are always appeals procedures and you and your supervisor should work out what to do next.

I emphasise that failure is very, very rare in PhDs, mainly because there is a series of hurdles that you have to jump over that ensure you can only submit a thesis for which your research is both adequate and convincing. If your thesis contains two or three new conclusions based on good experiments and solid, statistically validated conclusions about which your supervisor is basically happy, you should have no serious problems. If you have already published a refereed paper or two that have been bound into your thesis, you will know that some at least of your work is rock solid and this should give you confidence.

The reality is that >99% of people who submit a PhD thesis will get their degree. In contrast, 0% of people who do not submit a PhD thesis get their degree, no matter how long they have worked.

SECTION 4

POSTDOCS

CHAPTER 17: THE POSTDOC DECISION

As if you didn't have enough to do in the final year of your PhD, you have to confront what may be the most important questions in your academic year and perhaps your academic life: *Should I do a postdoc?* and, if so, *on what?* There are many good reasons for not doing a postdoc and here are some of them.

You will be entering on a long period of insecurity.

There are many fewer senior jobs in research and academe than potential applicants.

You are likely to end up in a worse institution than that at which you did your PhD.

Academic careers are very hard work and success in getting your own grants will demand an unsullied record of research success - there is never enough money for research.

If you really do not think that you are likely to succeed here, you should not try, but move sideways to industry (who often prefer to take on successful PhDs rather than failed postdocs), or to some other career where your transferable skills will give you an edge (see Chapter 20).

There are however good reasons for doing a postdoc and these include:

You like lab life and can let the long-term look after itself.

You know you are good enough to succeed in academe and research.

There is something that you want to understand better and nothing else matters.

The last reason is the one that is actually compelling: all scientists who envisage a future in research need to have something that drives them on, something that fascinates them, even if the rest of the world isn't much interested, preferably because they haven't realised its importance. It is this that will help them through the hard times that will certainly occur in the years to come.

Before you decide to do a postdoc, you will need to take a long cold look at yourself and your capabilities. Here, your CV will help you. Will it look impressive to the heads of major labs because, for example, it includes top degrees, prizes and publications? Will the references that you get impress their recipients? Will your technical abilities make you an immediately useful member of any lab that you join? The answers to these questions will tell you about the likelihood of your getting a postdoc in a good lab. If you fall below this standard, you should look for a postdoc only if your main concern is getting a reasonable job that you will enjoy, rather than having any long-term ambitions.

There are basically two types of postdocs: the majority are either dvertised or you hear about them on the grapevine from your supervisor or other PIs in your department; you then apply for them in the normal way. Eligibility here depends as much on technical competence and the ability that you have shown in being able to complete and publish work as anything else. You just see what is being advertised and apply for projects for which you are eligible in places that you might want to live. Postdocs in these positions are normally taken on to do a specific project and there are limited opportunities to initiate your own work, unless the PI sees your idea as fitting into the work defined within the grant that is paying your salary.

The second sort of postdoc results when you write to a PI saying that you would like to do a postdoc in their lab and give the reasons why. If your reasons, CV and references excite them sufficiently, and you can make the PI feel that your presence will do something good for their lab, they may create a postdoc position for you or allow you to follow in the steps of a postdoc who is leaving a position for which there is still funding. Things will go better here if the PI of a lab you contact knows your supervisor or someone else in your department working in their area and they will give you a good reference, ideally by phone or skype. Things will go even better if the new PI has met you at a meeting where you have presented a talk or poster or, even better, you have visited their lab and perhaps given a seminar. (***Hint****. If you foresee a career in research, make yourself known in your field as early as possible through contributions to meetings.*)

There is one other possibility which is to apply for a fellowship and so have your own money. On the one hand, this will allow you to go to any good lab in any university: your presence will carry prestige. On the other, you will be expected to produce good work instantly and move rapidly up the academic ladder. Once you have had a fellowship, it can be a bit tricky moving to a more standard postdoc, unless it is in a famous lab – you don't want to be seen as moving backwards. Unless you really are brilliant, it is probably better for your first position to be a postdoc in a good lab and this, you hope, will be a stepping stone to a fellowship.

What should be your new area of research?

This is the hardest question that you will confront and is far more important than the exact topic of your PhD, which was essentially made by your supervisor. This is the moment at which you really start to take control of your career. You have the choice of continuing in the area of your

PhD, moving sideways or entering a new area. If the former, you can have a discussion with your supervisor about good labs that you could move to and lines of research that are likely to be productive in the short to medium term (say over the next five years). It should however be said that, if these lines are too obvious, others will already be pursuing them.

There are strong reasons for moving to an adjacent area where your existing knowledge and skills will provide a solid baseline for your new work. Your potential PI might look very favourably on such an application because you will bring related expertise to their lab and not much time will be wasted in bringing you up to speed in your new department. As a result of your move, you will broaden and deepen your knowledge and skills and should be well positioned to decide on where you see yourself going in the longer term. Choosing the lab for a second postdoc should be straightforward.

If you do, however, choose to change subject completely, this will probably be because you have come to feel that your existing area of research is running out of steam and excitement. No one can help you find a new field, but you will almost certainly have discovered it for yourself. In practice, the stimulus for the move will have come from attending a talk by a well-known scientist who has done something that excited you in a system you had barely been aware of (this is what happened to me when I moved from biophysics to developmental biology). You will have followed up this talk through reading and attending seminars, had conversations with other people in the new field, and slowly begun to focus in on the problems that you want to solve.

If you do decide to make such a major leap, you will not have been the first person to do so: many people with, for example, PhDs in physics and chemistry or degrees in medicine have made wonderful contributions to biology. But beware: you will have a steep learning curve as you have not only to bring yourself up to speed in a new subject, but also immerse yourself in a culture where you know nobody. It is the most risky option, but it is also the most exciting one. If you do go down this path, however, do be a bit careful and not appear arrogant to your new colleagues who will, at least at the beginning, know a lot more than you about your new area.

What matters at this stage is that you find an area to which you really feel committed and whose importance may be underestimated. You now need to find a range of labs that focus on your new interests. Glance through the publications coming out of these labs and decide on a shortlist of those that look impressive and that are in places you might want to go to. You also need to find someone in your own university who knows about this field and make an appointment to talk to them. This should help you to shorten that short list of labs to contact.

Your letter of application will not be straightforward to write: you will need to emphasise your wonderful academic record and your excitement about their work as well the useful skills that you will bring with you. If there is nothing that you can do there that would be productive, there is no reason for them to take you on. If you really do want to switch fields and preliminary applications are not promising, there is an alternative route. You should do a first postdoc in a field that is intermediate between where you are now and where you hope to be, ideally in a university that is strong in the field that you want to enter. There, you can make a point of learning about that new area, making contacts and developing the skills that will be useful in that new field, while still doing productive and publishable work.

Then, when you apply for that second postdoc, you will have a good story to tell about how you made a commitment to the new field two years earlier and have worked successfully to bring yourself up to speed in it. One approach here is to see the PI of a potential second lab in the final year of your PhD and ask them for advice about the stepping-stone postdoc that they would recommend before they would consider you. It always pays to make contact with academics if there is a good reason to do so, and they will certainly remember you later. Indeed, if that first

How to Become a Scientist

postdoc is in the same university as that of the second PI, you can keep in contact with their lab and go to relevant seminars. In this way, you will both show commitment and give yourself an inside advantage for any future postdoc positions that may become available.

This chapter started off with a binary choice, whether you should or should not do a postdoc. You should not make a final decision too soon. If you have any doubts, start by thinking about a postdoc as you can always abandon the effort or even a job that you have accepted if you start to have major and serious doubts about this choice of career (although this will not make you popular with the lab you reject). There are relatively few labs in the world that focus on your interests, while there are many, many more opportunities outside of academe.

CHAPTER 18: APPLYING FOR A POSTDOC

It usually takes longer than you might expect to get a postdoctoral position. This is because few labs have the necessary funding on tap or because a position that is funded doesn't become vacant for some time. If that lab has to apply for funds, the whole process can take many months, with no guarantee that the application will be successful. Given the eccentricities of getting funding support, you should have a shortlist of labs that you would be happy to go to and apply to all of them at least six months before you want to go there.

Even if a funding application is successful, it is quite common for the grant not to start until after your student funding has run out. In that case, your first approach is to ask your supervisor whether there might be some bridging money to cover you over the period between when your student funding ends and a postdoc starts. If you find yourself in this position, you should mention what technical work you could do for the lab over this period while you are preparing the papers from your thesis for publication. Although you may only get three months of support, this should be enough for you get your papers submitted. Even if your supervisor has no spare funds, there may be short-term support in another lab in your department where you can be technically useful while you finish your papers.

How should you apply for a postdoc?

If you want is a position in the general area of your current research and have identified the lab that you want to go to, you should email your potential PI, attaching your CV and ask them if a postdoctoral position is likely to arise in their lab soon, saying that you would be happy to visit them. Here, mentioning the likely title of your thesis may elicit an invitation to give a talk, so it is probably not wise to go down this route until you do have a talk to give. You should also mention your plans to your supervisor, and they may well contact the PI informally to talk about you.

It can sometimes happen that such a talk or, perhaps, a discussion over a poster at a meeting can lead to an informal offer of a postdoc position. If this happens and you are enthusiastic about the possibility, say that you will email them about it (note whether you get a positive response here). You should then email the potential PI saying where you met, their mention of a postdoc position and that you are interested in following this up and why. You should attach your CV to this email, having first checked that your interests as detailed in the CV at least mesh with that of the PI's lab. What is key here is that every subsequent step in the process is documented so that both sides know where they are[10].

If you are applying for a postdoc in a field that is not directly related to that of your thesis, you need to tread more carefully. Your email has to imply not only that you have become fascinated by their area and line of research (and your email should demonstrate that you have that knowledge) but that you would bring useful technical expertise to the lab. Here, for your request to carry weight, you really do need to have an impressive CV and references. You might also say that, even if they have no postdoc position available now, you would appreciate an opportunity to visit the lab and talk to people there, and this might be possible at a time that you are nearby because you will be attending a meeting. Make it easy for them to invite you because you can never be sure what unexpected opportunities might arise from meeting new people in a new field.

If you are applying for a fellowship, part of the application will probably include the details of the lab that you hope to work in. As the deadlines for such applications are often many months in advance of any award, you may have to apply to labs earlier than you would like. You may therefore have to contact these labs some nine months before you want to go there. While you will want to go to the lab to learn, they will have to want to accept you as a guest, which essentially is what a fellowship is. They will consequently need to see what you want to do, why you want to do it and how good you are. As you will not have completed your PhD work and are unlikely to have much in the way of publications, they will only want you if your CV is stellar and your thesis is likely to have been submitted before the starting date of the position. This is why it is usually better and easier to apply for a fellowship after you have done a first postdoc.

Finally, wherever you are preparing to apply for a postdoc, stand back and consider whether being at that lab in that university is likely to enhance your CV. While top universities carry name-recognition kudos, the most important criterion is that the new PI and their lab are *currently* publishing good research in good journals. It will be much easier for you to publish in that environment than in one that is, even if only temporarily, publication quiescent. It is that steady flow of papers that you intend to publish that will lubricate your path to a research career.

CHAPTER 19: SUCCEEDING AS A POSTDOC

You will start your postdoc with one simple aim, to do well; but this aim has many components. Here are some of them.

Do high-quality research work that you can publish, and soon.

Learn some new techniques.

Expand your knowledge, particularly if the lab is in a new area for you.

Become part of the culture of the new lab.

Expand your network of contacts, particularly through collaborating with other labs.

Improve your public profile through talks and posters at meetings.

Develop your own ideas and start to develop some independence.

All of these aims have a further importance: they will expand your CV and improve the likelihood of getting a further and perhaps better postdoc. We can look at each in turn.

Research work

Ideally, your contract will be for three years and you will have a little time to relax into your new post. If, however, it is a two-year position, you will need to hit the ground running and the easiest way to do this is to become part of an existing project for which your technical background adds something that the new lab needs. You should suggest to your PI that you do something along these lines while you get yourself into the main project for which you were taken on. Working on someone else's problem will not only help you become part of the new lab but, with luck, will also earn you minor authorship on their paper(s). At this early stage in your career, others will look at your publication record and secondary authorship on papers not only lengthen your publication list but show that you are a good colleague.

As to your own project, the difference between postdoctoral and postgraduate work is that PIs assume that you have the technical repertoire and the intellectual heft to take full responsibility with relatively little input from them. Indeed, you may be the only person in the lab who knows some of the techniques that you will need. It is also assumed that you are capable of learning any new techniques that may be required, although some may require tuition. Even if you are moving to a new area, your PI will assume that you will need no more than casual guidance in what you do as you are a proven, if relatively inexperienced, scientist. The downside of all this is that it is you who are responsible for developing your postdoc skills.

What will help you in your research is what helped you in your postgraduate work: having clearly formulated questions and hypotheses that need answering and testing. Your initial discussions with you new PI should focus on these as they will help to get you going and structure your time at the bench. It is, however, the sophistication of thinking that you bring to the project that distinguishes you from a postgraduate student.

What marks out postdocs who are likely to have a future in science is the degree of control that they show that they are able to exert over their project, the strength of their intellectual approach and their ability to produce ideas that be experimentally tested. These are abilities that you will be expected to show fairly rapidly if you want, as you should, your PI to leave matters in your hands. You will, of course, want to keep in contact with them about what you are doing through regular discussions and lab meetings. Being a postdoc means taking responsibility!

Learn some new techniques

You should aim to broaden your technical repertoire by learning everything that this lab does that your previous lab didn't, and the best way here is to be involved in a project that needs these skills and to use some of them yourself.

Expand your knowledge, particularly if the lab is in a new area for you

This is an obvious aim if the lab is in a new area. In this case, you really do need to do the basic reading that everyone who is already in the area takes for granted. This is particularly important because, as your background is in a different area, you will be hoping to bring a new perspective to the field. This will not come because you can read the current literature better than anyone else, you almost certainly cannot. What you should be hoping for is that, by looking at the phenomena and the earlier work with new eyes, you will see interesting questions that more established research workers will not have thought about.

Become part of the culture of the new lab

You need to become part of the lab rapidly, both for academic and for social reasons, particularly if you have come to a new town where you have no social support. What helps here is being seen as collaborative as well as being friendly. This is where your technical and other transferable skills will be useful, particularly your statistical and programming abilities. You should also be interested in the other projects going on in the lab; this is a good way both of becoming known and of finding out more about a new field.

Expand your network of contacts and collaborators

If you are in a new department, go to all the seminars, at the beginning at least. One reason for this is that you may feel that your project needs some technique not done in your lab but may perhaps be used elsewhere in the department. Knowing what is going on in other labs may prove helpful as well as interesting.

Collaborations are always worthwhile provided the collaborators bring different skills to a question which both want to answer. These go particularly well if neither is far more senior than the others so you can see one another as essentially equals. Take every opportunity of collaborating with people in your own and in other labs (who knows where you will want a job in the future?). Do however make sure that your PI knows what you are doing. They are, after all, paying your salary and their first interest is that you have time to complete what you were taken on to do.

Improve your public profile through talks and posters at meetings

You will need to start building a public profile for yourself in the field, so go to local meetings, present talks and posters and join the appropriate scientific society. Apart from the opportunity to get to know other postdocs in fields related to your own, it will offer opportunities for getting grants to go to prestigious meetings.

Any grants that you do obtain will be gold dust on your CV: these can be awarded for travel, for consumables, for equipment and for living costs. (***Hint***: *Apply for grants as, to anyone reading your CV, success here indicates talent and initiative*.)

Become an independent scientist

What marks out postdocs who have a serious future in science is that they start to think deeply about their own area, getting insights into what is known, what is not known and what matters. These are the scientists who will be thinking about applying for stand-alone fellowships and developing their own lines of research. If your ideas are good enough and relevant enough to the interests of the lab, your PI may give you sufficient support to allow you to work on them. Indeed, they should always be prepared to allow you a little time to work on your own ideas, provided you can still do what you are employed to do.

It should be said that many postdocs have done some of their own work on the side and never bothered to mention it to their PI. If you do however go down that road, it may prove counterproductive to give talks outside of the lab or to consider publishing this work without first discussing it with your PI. Such constraints do not of course apply to publishing your earlier PhD research. Here, all you need to do is to give your original and current lab addresses, although it is polite to mention progress here to your PI.

What matters for your career is that you publish a paper or two a year while you are a postdoc. If all else fails, you can always write a review on some timely topic, and, if it useful, you may be surprised and pleased at how many citations it will receive. The importance of first-authorship and especially single-author papers as a postdoc is that they provide hard evidence that you are capable of taking the lead and being responsible for research projects.

The first year

After six months, you should have become a valued member of your new lab, producing results of publishable quality that answer the questions that got you going, and having learnt more than you would have thought possible. With luck, you will have contributed material to ongoing papers, and you can relax because you know that things have gone reasonably well, even if you are tired.

During the second six months, you will be focusing on the project you came to do and making it your own through having found what lines of research are working and which are less profitable. You should have answered some of the initial questions and come up with more of your own. By now, your PI, who will have followed your progress in lab meetings and private discussions, should have learnt to trust you and give your head. By the end of the year, and with just a little luck you will be on your way to a publication, probably in collaboration with another postdoc or senior graduate student and maybe others, probably with your PI as the corresponding author.

The second and subsequent years

You are now becoming a scientist with some experience and may even be helping look after graduate and honours students (more for the CV!). You should be taking the initiative in planning your lab work and thinking about publishing some research and perhaps a review with your PI. With just a little luck, you will feel that you are on the right track and are becoming seriously interested in a research career.

If you have a three-year position, the aims for the second year are to do as much research as possible making sure that you have both short-term and long-term ambitions. That extra year will allow you to take on a risky project that is exciting, knowing that you are also doing some other research which, although it may be more mundane, is highly likely to be productive. It is important that you test yourself in the lab and find out if you are able to produce good and interesting ideas, some of which at least will work. If you cannot do this, move away from thinking about a pure research career, even if you are competent in the lab.

Something of this also applies even if you have a two-year position. Here, you inevitably have to focus on shorter-term ambitions, but you should still be thinking about exciting projects. With luck you can do the basic work for them now, knowing that any results will be useful later, particularly if you have to put forward an impressive and well-founded project for a fellowship application. As I wrote earlier, one's best work is done in one's head and thinking deeply about an area one really cares about is exciting; it is what drives us on. You must be able to spend time being imaginative if you want a career in academic research.

When you only have about nine months left on your contract, you will need to start working on what to do next.

CHAPTER 20: ALTERNATIVE CAREERS

If you are beginning to feel that a research career in academe is not for you, either because you sense that the chances of future success are not high (too many postdocs chasing too few academic positions) or because your time as a postdoc has been less than ideal, what should you do? The first thing is not to despair! There are plenty of research and other jobs outside of academe and many of them have better pay and better prospects than academic ones, so you shouldn't worry too much.

The one thing you should not do under these circumstances is to stop working hard, even if your postdoc position has become a job rather than part of a vocation. This is because the things that will help you get a job in non-academic science or even outside of science are publications and a good reference. Research-based companies, publishers and the civil service, for example, are much more likely to be sympathetic to taking on an applicant with a purely academic background if that person has already shown themselves hard-working, energetic and talented than someone who sees themselves as just not up to an academic job (wouldn't you?).

The key thing is to work through what you want to do next, bearing in mind that your academic and research skills really are useful in the wider world. You have good degrees, you can read quickly, you can write and speak in public, you are far more competent with computers and statistics than most people and you are clever. It should not be too difficult to refocus your CV away from academe and make it look good and appropriate for other lines of work.

The next thing to do is to visit the Careers Department in your university and talk to them on the realities of life in the areas that interest you. They will probably give you good advice. If you want to remain in science but see yourself working in industry, there may be local spin-off companies that need people with your talents. If you like academic science but don't feel that the insecurity of life as a PI is for you, another option is lab administration: all big labs need someone to run the lab on a day-to-day basis, rather than focus solely on the scientific programme. No matter what you think will suit you, the Careers people should be able to point you in the right direction.

Once things are clear in your head, you know that you are going to leave academe and have a sense of where you will be going, you need to talk to your PI. You will want to discuss how your remaining time in the lab can be of greatest use to them and the lab (there is no point in being selfish here) and also, if you want to move to industry, whether they have any advice or contacts you can approach. A professional approach here should pay dividends when you want a reference.

At this stage, if not before, you should start looking for jobs - it should not be an ambition to have no source of income when your postdoc funding runs out! The Careers Department will give you some advice on how to approach companies and other organisations. When you do talk to prospective employers, you must be positive, focusing on your genuine interest about the new area and not grumbling about the past. You need to be seen as being ready to move on.

On a more general note, every postdoc approaching the last six months of their first postdoc should ask themselves whether they want a career in academe, and before answering it should look around and see what has happened to good postdocs they have known after they have completed a second postdoc. My guess is that, unless they are in a rapidly expanding field such as computer science, a fair proportion of them are not progressing anything like as rapidly as they might have hoped. After a second postdoc, you will certainly be in your '30s and the idea of further short-term postdocs with no natural career progression is not an attractive option.

If you feel that your likely chances of long-term academic success are not high and this matters to you, you really should be thinking about alternative careers. It is easier to do this after a first than a second postdoc when you will inevitably be seen as someone who is not good enough for academe and who may be too specialised and senior as a research worker to slot into an alternative research career easily. You may also have to accept a lower salary than your current one. If you have any doubts about your future in academe, you will lose nothing by having a preliminary and informal discussion with the Careers Department. It will give you the chance to compare the possible alternative careers "out there" with the straight academic path.

CHAPTER 21: SECOND POSTDOCS, FELLOWSHIPS AND BEYOND

Once you are certain that you want to stay in academe if you possibly can, you will need to think about applying for a second postdoc or a fellowship. The first decision to be made is whether to stay where you are or move to a new lab, and you should be making this decision early in your final year. If you do want to stay where you are, you should have a discussion with your PI about your future and you may get a good idea about whether there is a good chance of your staying on or whether they will want you to move. If you feel that you want to move, you should do some serious thinking about the area of research in which you want to work and start looking for possible labs.

Staying where you are

There are advantages to staying where you are:

> You know the lab, the department the university and the town.
>
> You may well have a partner who is loath to move and staying is easier for the relationship.
>
> You are doing projects that are going well and don't want to hand them over.
>
> There are papers in progress, and you aren't ready to move.
>
> As a senior postdoc, you will start to take on real responsibilities in the lab (more for your CV).
>
> If you are publishing regularly and things are going well, you will have started to build a reputation in your department. Hence, if there are academic or proper research jobs coming up in your area, you know that you will almost certainly be shortlisted because the appointment committee will see you as "safe".

If you decide that you would like to stay where you are, you need to talk to your PI at least nine months before your money runs out to ask about the chances of there being funding for a second postdoc. If they are enthusiastic, they may be willing in principle, but tell you that the position will need new funding. If you are lucky, they will ask what you want to do and to start drafting a grant application for the work that you will do rather than taking the initiative themselves. Although this will give you more work, you will be given a lesson in one of the advanced skills that all academics need: how to write a convincing grant application (see Chapter 33). You might also discuss with your PI alternatives that you could pursue if the application is not successful, and key here are other labs with whom the PI has a good working relationship.

Moving to a new lab

There are some strong arguments for moving to a new lab, particularly if things have gone well and you have published some good papers.

You will gain new experiences and skills.

You may feel that you need to move on as you are unlikely to learn anything new if you stay where you are.

Your interests are shifting away from those of your PI, and if you don't follow them now, you may never get the opportunity.

A new lab may be more prestigious and will look good on your CV.

Moving is the riskier but more exciting option, particularly if you are thinking about a lab whose PI has real international status. Postdocs in such labs are, however, very competitive and your CV needs to show that you really are someone on the way up, with a body of published papers, if you are even to get to the interview stage. Such PIs only want good people in their labs because they aim to remain at the top of their field. If you are accepted in such a lab, you may be surprised at how competitive it is there. On the other hand, being in that lab will look good on your CV, while the tensions there may prepare you better for a future life in research than somewhere a little sleepier.

What is very hard to do at this stage is to change subjects completely. You may be able to get a second postdoc in a lab whose interests have hitherto not been yours, but it will be because of your technical skills and perhaps because, although they have money, no one in their own field has applied. If your CV shows too much chopping and changing, it carries the implication that you are not a serious person with real interests. The one good reason for doing this is that you have become seriously interested in an area that bridges the lab of your first postdoc with that in the second and you are applying to the new lab for the very best of scientific reasons, even though your background is in another area (see Chapter 17).

For your arguments to be convincing here, you will need to show that what you want to do not only makes scientific sense and that you have done the reading to show that you are committed, but that you can fulfil a useful role in the new lab. Your chances of being taken on will depend on the strength of you CV and the academic weight of your proposal. Oddly enough, this sort of a case may be far more convincing to a top lab than a more standard one: the best labs are always on the lookout for new and exciting lines of work, particularly those that involve their own methodologies and interests. As such labs are usually far better funded than others, they may be able to find you a postdoc position, but you will need to prove yourself by giving a very good interview talk. This will have to explain how you see your own expertise meshing with theirs in a way that is scientifically beneficial.

If you decide that do you want to move, you do not need to tell your current PI about your plans until you have contacted potential PIs either as a reply to advertisements or have sent them an email (attaching your CV) explaining your interest and asking if there is likely to be a position in their lab for which you can apply. If you do get encouraging responses, however, you should tell your PI immediately, if for no other reason that the new lab head is likely to phone your supervisor for an informal reference. You should also try to visit such labs to see if they are what you want and to give them an opportunity to decide if you are what they want.

At this point, your current PI will realise that you are thinking about leaving their lab and this will change the nature of your relationship. As no decisions have been made, you can say that you are not sure as to whether there will be a future for you in their lab and that you are testing the waters. You do not want to exclude possibilities too soon. You should also emphasise that, if you do leave, you have every intention of ensuring that your project is left in a publishable state and with drafts of the papers completed (you should always leave a laboratory with no major writing-up responsibilities). It is important here that you stay on good terms with your supervisor as, even if you leave, they will still be needed for references. It is always far better that they remain a colleague and a mentor than that they forget about you.

Fellowships

Postdocs who are good enough to find their own areas of work are in the class of scientists who are strong enough to apply for competitive fellowships, particularly if others are likely to feel that any application you submit shows real signs of originality. If you think that you are up to it, then search for funded fellowships and download the application forms as soon as possible, ideally several months before any deadlines. You can look at the forms and decide if you are the sort of person who might be eligible, *and you should always give yourself the benefit of any doubt*! Fellowships are only given to people who apply, and you can have no sense of the competition: you may think that you not are up to it, but that is not a decision for you. Indeed, it is often worth applying for the experience of producing the application as this will force you to produce an interesting project. And

How to Become a Scientist

once you have applied, who knows what can happen? It should also be said that, if you are applying for one fellowship, you may as well submit applications for several to improve your chances – it won't be much extra work.

You are now going to be particularly busy because, at the same time that you are doing your postdoctoral research and, hopefully, writing papers, you have to formulate a clever research project (see Chapter 33). You need to give yourself a couple of months or so to do this as you will need to think deeply about the roots of your subject and aspects of it that remain unknown. For the fellowship application, you will be required to name the laboratory in which you intend to work. You therefore will need to decide who are the best people in the field of your proposed work and then contact them. The email should include the request, your CV, an abstract of the work you want to do and the reasons why you want to come to their lab. Here, the chances of being accepted are quite good, first because you will bring your own money and second because the details in the request should show that you are in the top echelon of young scientists.

To be shortlisted for a fellowship, you will need a very good CV together with referees who will imply that you have the ability and originality that they are looking for. You will however only get that fellowship if you can convince a panel of very good scientists that what you want to do with the fellowship is both interesting and original and that you have serious scientific potential. Think very carefully about the project that you want to do, the reasons for doing it and why the results should be interesting in both the immediate and wider contexts. Producing such a project is, to say the least, challenging. The situation may, however, be easier (standards may be lower) if applications for the fellowship are restricted (e.g. to people within the university or to, say, a particular social group).

You should however be aware that fellowships, because they carry money and prestige, are highly competitive and almost all applicants will fail. This not only means that you need to apply for several fellowships if you can, but that you also have to think about alternative labs to whom you can apply for a second postdoc. Always have a plan B, a plan C and a plan D!

And beyond!
If you are at this stage in your career, you should know about the possible career options. What follows is really aimed at people on lower rungs of the academic ladder who want to know more about the higher ones.

If, towards the end of a second postdoc or a fellowship, you decide that you want to stay in research for your career, you will need to choose whether your priority is an academic position in a university or a position in a research institute that has no undergraduate teaching (what to do if you feel that this life is not for you is covered in Chapter 20). Although it may be possible to stay where you are, and you will then probably be running the lab at this stage, people tend to do this only if it is a clear and short-term step on the way to a higher position in that department or institute. You should, in general, only look for a third full postdoc position if you see your career as being a senior research assistant or lab administrator rather than an independent scientist or an academic in a good university.

If you have shown that your research career is progressing well and you want to pusue a career in pure science, then you will need to contact your friends and scan advertisements in journals and on the websites of the major research institutes in your field, and you will have to go where there is a position. Good research institutes often operate on the hotel principle: they take on senior postdocs, either with their own funding for as long as it lasts, or providing support for them and a small lab for five or six-years. Such institutes sometimes offer the possibility of a second such contract, but few offer longer-term prospects.

When your time runs out, they will replace you with a younger postdoc, usually in a new area of research. There are always clever and ambitious younger postdocs who want jobs, and they will be cheaper than you to employ. If, however, your time at the hotel has gone well and been productive, you will then be in an excellent position to be taken on in a university or other research institute in a permanent position. If so, you are still likely to need external funding to top up the basic support that comes with the job.

There may also be more advanced fellowships for which you can apply. These have the advantage that you can take them to most places, but your application will not be strengthened if the lab to which you want to take it is not internationally known.

The other choice is a lectureship or assistant professorship in a university. These are, as is everything else at this stage, highly competitive. Once you have been appointed, the department will require you to set up your lab and get your own research funding at the same time as or soon after you are starting to teach. You will be very busy, and some young academics never get properly off the ground. The easiest route, and often the most successful one, is to join a department where there is a considerable amount of research already going on in your general area. You will then start with academic colleagues and facilities and perhaps someone who is happy to give you space in their lab while you are getting your own funding and equipment.

The one feature of life in all universities is that there are many other things going on apart from research, and this is a very mixed blessing. One implication is that you may have to fight to ensure that you have sufficient time for your own research as you will be asked to teach, supervise student lab projects (a cheap way of getting preliminary work done!) and handle administrative stuff (sit on committees, handle admissions, become responsible for health and safety or radioactivity or something even less interesting). The amount of administration in a university is terrifying. One solution to this pressure is to be so brilliant at research, measured by grants, papers and studentships, that the department protects your research time to keep its reputation.

All of this non-research stuff does have its uses. If you begin to feel that your research career is flagging and that getting research grants is becoming harder and harder, there are alternative roles to take on in a university. In later life, many academics find a satisfying career in teaching and even administration. In the latter case, the trick is to work out early what branch of administration suits you and start helping there, before your head of department tells you to do something else. By taking on more teaching and administration, you will also know that you are facilitating the path of science because you will be protecting the research time of your younger colleagues.

SECTION 5

CONCLUSIONS

CHAPTER 22: LUCK

Over the years, you will probably have had a fair amount of luck, good and bad, defined as things happening that you could never have expected. What is often underestimated is how important is the role that luck plays in a scientific career. This short chapter is on how to improve your chances of minimising the chances of bad luck and improving your chances of getting good luck.

Some examples of bad luck are beyond your control. I have known students and postdocs whose supervisors have died leaving them academically isolated at a crucial time. A next-door lab burnt down with the result that a year of work for some twenty people was lost, together with some of their data that had been stored on their computers. Crucial pieces of expensive kit have died and there has been no money to replace them. Another lab has published the research you have been working on for two years (there are several stories of maths students having to abandon their postgraduate work because someone proved the conjecture on which they had been working for some years).

The only way of guaranteeing survival against such disasters is to be sufficiently paranoid to believe that everything will fail, and that you always have to have a set of secondary alternatives – but this is no way to live your life in research.

Table 22.1 lists some ways to avoid bad luck. Examples are: As to getting good luck, the key is to put yourself in a place where good luck happens, and there are two helpful ways of doing this. First is to work on a project where not that much is known: here, you will have room for discovery. Indeed, it is a good bet that, if you study some well-known phenomenon with a new technique, you will discover something new. All research projects should include an element of this. Second is to be in a productive lab, one whose supervisor and earlier students and postdocs have a good track record of publication. Ideally, this lab should be in a well-known department in a university whose presence in your CV guarantees name recognition.

Table 22.1 Ways to avoid the risk of bad luck
1: Working on several projects simultaneously that do

How to Become a Scientist

not depend on a single idea alone in case that idea was wrong.

2: Planning your experiments so that, if something goes wrong with one, there are other, more profitable lines of work in progress, even if they are only thesis-fodder.

3: Reviewing negative results in case they might be positive in the light of a different premise.

4: Not drawing your early experiments too tightly so that, if they fail, you have nothing.

5: Making sure that your research does not depend on a single piece of equipment.

6: Making sure that you have collaborations with other labs.

7: Having a second supervisor in case there are crises with your main one or their lab.

8: Always, always backing up your computer files in the cloud.

But beware: luck is odd and fickle. You should know that being in places where work has always gone well carries its own risks. I once had to write a professorial reference for someone with such a track record. Looking through their CV, it soon became clear that this was a person who had done lovely work as a postdoc in very good labs, but, once they had started their own lab, the quality of their work had dropped markedly. This was because they had never really developed serious ideas of their own, probably because they had never had to.

199

It is sometimes said that, the harder you work, the luckier you get, but I am not sure that this actually applies to young scientists. What really matters is having good ideas and these can come as easily from dreaming as from slaving at the bench. But you do have to have something to dream about, so you must set aside time for thinking. Even more important is recognising when you have had good luck and then making the most of it. There is not a lot of good luck around, but careers, even Nobel prizes, have resulted when scientists have recognised their good fortune and built on it. Table 22.2 lists some other pointers to putting yourself in a place where good luck can happen and how to recognise it.

Table 22.2. Ways to increase your chances of being lucky

1: Spend time thinking about your area and wider subject, looking for gaps in knowledge and understanding. If something interesting emerges from the ether, think and dream about it before being critical. The latter is easy, the former is hard but is a habit you should get yourself into.

2: If you get an unexpected result whereby something happens that shouldn't have or *vice versa*, always ask yourself what is going on. Normally, the answer is trivial, but occasionally it isn't. *This is the most important sort of luck to get – miss it at your peril.*

3: Go to seminars not directly relevant to your research, particularly those given by scientists with a serious reputation. You never know when you will pick up knowledge or insights that may help your work or that will excite you and make you think.
4: Get to know what is going on in other labs, and for the same reason.
5: Make friends in other departments and universities, for the same reason; in addition, you might hear about potential job opportunities. This is a key advantage of having made an international network of friends when you were an undergraduate and PhD student. If you want a job in their area, contact them.
6: Be aware of the development of any new techniques in your university or institute and wonder whether they could usefully be applied to your work.
7: When you move to a new institution, find out what is going on outside of your immediate lab.
8: Take on responsibilities that are not directly related to your research. You never know where they will lead or what further opportunities you may hear about when you are mixing with people outside of your lab.

***Hint:** Two of the greatest sins in science are (i) not to recognise good luck when it comes your way and (ii) not to make the most of it when you do realise what is happening.*

Good luck is rare, but not that rare: I can immediately think of six times when taking advantage of simple good luck has given my career a major lift. Indeed, I might have failed as a scientist if I hadn't taken advantage of the first three occasions. The fourth was giving a bad seminar as part of a postdoc application. I was rejected, but found another far better lab in the same town that was prepared to take me on, and I did far more interesting and useful work there than I could possibly have done in the first one. I can also think of three times when I made very bad decisions – but perhaps that was stupidity rather than bad luck.

There are two ways to avoid making stupid decisions: first, sleep on those decisions before committing yourself and, second, discuss them with other people. If you have a serious choice to make, you might also do what Darwin did when he was considering marrying his cousin: he wrote down a list of the pros and the cons of marriage. He clearly came to the right decision because he had many happy years with Emma.

In short, if you do at least the minimum to avoid bad luck and you keep an eye out for opportunities which may lead to good luck, things should more than even out.

You may however find that the best luck is that which you make for yourself. Science is an odd business and you will never read about many of the positions that would suit you. So, if you are visiting another lab and it turns out that they have nothing for you now, never hesitate to ask questions along the lines of

> If there is nothing in your lab, might there be something coming up in my general area in this department/university/neighbourhood. I am keen to come to this area because, say, my partner has a job nearby.
>
> Do you know of anyone else working in this general research area who might be looking for a postdoc?

You never know what the reply might be!

So far, this book has mainly been about the orthodox, canonical route to becoming a scientist. It is not the only way. Many considerable scientists have started off doing other things: Ed Witten, for example, is a great theoretical physicist even though his first degree was in history and linguistics. Fritz London, the theoretical chemist, got an MSc in philosophy before he moved to science. Other scientists have worked their way up after starting as a technician. What they all had in common was a fascination for the unknown in nature. If you share this fascination, you should try to follow your instincts and badger universities and labs to take you on in some capacity. You never know when or if you will strike lucky, but you can be absolutely sure that, if you don't try, you certainly won't.

CHAPTER 23: A LIFE IN SCIENCE

If you have read all of this book, you will have realised that the path to becoming a professional scientist with a good chance of success in academe is not an easy one to progress along. While many will want to start on that path, it gets narrower and narrower and, sad to say, only a smallish fraction of those starting out will achieve their implicit ambition of becoming a professor in a leading research university. Fortunately, there are side-roads to other opportunities on the way, whether you have an MSc, a PhD or a postdoctoral position, and many of them have better prospects and rewards than a life in academe or research.

The good news therefore is that there is no reason not to start off down that path if you like doing and thinking about science. There is a great deal of pleasure in solving research problems, even small ones. Working in research and burying you head in the minutiae of experimentation is a wonderful distraction from the complexities of work, administration and life. Writing papers is hard, but seeing the completed publication in print or on the screen always gives one a sense of pride and achievement.

If you do feel that you are good at scientific research and decide that the risks don't matter and this is what you want to do, there are many benefits that come with a life in academe. One is teaching both postgraduates and undergraduates. The interactions we have with our students are not only a pleasure, but an education for us as well: teaching forces us to think deeply about our subject and that often carries its own benefits. If we are lucky, our students will do better than us and we can profit from their fresh and original minds, and we can encourage that luck by inspiring them to be clever. The relationship between a supervisor and a postgraduate or postdoc has some similarities between a parent and child. They start off by needing you, but less and less as time goes by so that, after a few years, you and they are colleagues and eventually academic equals. Later, the original relationship reverses and they overtake you, and you can take great pride in their successes.

There are international benefits to an academic life and that is the opportunity not only to make friends in your own country but, because science is so international, with scientists from other countries whom you will meet in labs and at meetings. When they go home, you have the beginnings of an international set of colleagues and friends, something that will happen to few outside of academe. There are also opportunities to spend time in laboratories in other countries, as a student a postdoc or as a visitor.

Being a research scientist is not however an easy life: you will spend evenings and weekends poring over papers, going back to the lab to check experiments, writing papers, preparing grants, reviewing papers and marking student work. Being a scientist is as much a way of life as it is a job. If you want regular hours and a good salary, do something easier.

If, however, there is something in nature that fascinates you and you are driven to sort it out, no matter how difficult it is, this research ambition may sustain you through all the hurdles you will have to jump over as you progress from your first degree to the giddy heights of being a professor. It will be hard, unless you are, and are seen to be brilliant – in which case, fellowships and jobs will come your way. It has to be said that early brilliance is generally rare in the experimental sciences, but is more common in the maths-based theoretical sciences. One reason for this is that a theoretician can work on their own, needing little more than a computer and colleagues.

It is a consolation to the rest of us that, while theoreticians show early talent, they risk burning out prematurely; in contrast, those in the experimental sciences often don't get into their stride until their '30s, and the best ones keep doing good work for decades. The point to remember is that you need to find an area that you care about and is important to you; you can then develop it and make it your own. That is the real key to success in science, and its great joy.

SECTION 5

TRANSFERABLE SKILLS

Transferable skills are, as the name indicates, those skills which you will need throughout your life in science, irrespective of your topic and wherever you go. Most of them are as useful outside of academe as they are taken for granted within it. Some are concerned with public behaviour (e.g. speaking and chairing), others with academic abilities (e.g. grant applications and statistics). Ensure you develop them as they will give you confidence, while their absence make you look amateur, and this is never a good thing. Once, you are a doctoral student, you are responsible for continuing your own education so make sure you do so.

CHAPTER 24: WRITING A CV

The keys to a noteworthy CV are that (1) the reader rapidly gets the points that assure them that you are the sort of person that they want to take on and (2) it looks good in the sense that its appearance carries a message of competence. The covering letter of application should also look good, but needs to be short as it is the CV that will get you an interview.

If you are applying for a PhD studentship, you should assume that every other applicant has a good honours degree. If you are applying for a postdoc position, you should assume that every other applicant has a PhD or will have one soon. All applications are competitive and what will mark out your CV is what extra it contains beyond your degrees. For a PhD position, research experience and prizes are gold dust. For a postdoc position, what will mark you out are research publications, ideally in refereed journals. For both, grant awards, even for academic travel, are also important. If you have any of these, they, together with prizes. should be in a prominent position. If you haven't been awarded any grants, try and get them, and as soon as possible. CVs need to impress readers!

What looks good is however subject-dependant: if you are applying for a job in advertising, the reader will look for artistic flair. Things are a bit more mundane in science as we tend to distrust anything that looks flashy, so don't take the risk. What we like is something that is easy and pleasant to read, and doesn't look cramped, fussy or untidy. If spacing the text means that the CV requires more pages, that is good because you can hide more modest achievements in the middle: most attention is paid to the front page and the end, where you will list the names of your referees.

For the text, I'd recommend a neat, modern, san-serif font such as Calibri, using 12 point for the text, with bold headings and italic subheadings. Normally, single spacing with a 6-point gap between paragraphs will look fine, but you may prefer 1.5x spacing. Ideally, topics should not over-run pages as it looks fussy, so you can use any resulting empty space on a page to make the text look good to the eye. Including a photograph makes the CV look more personal, but its presence is not necessary. If you do include a photograph, make sure you look reasonably professional. The key thing is that, once it is finished, you should feel that the CV represents you and your achievements in a way that makes you pleased.

The order in which you include material is up to you, but the following is as good as any. The list of topics below is quite long, and one would not expect a PhD applicant to require all of them. If, however, you are applying for a second postdoc or a fellowship, almost all of them should be needed. One reason for including so many topics is to show you the wide range of opportunities that there are for young scientists and to encourage you to go for them.

CV Sections.

Personal details: These should include your name, age, date of birth, nationality, home and work addresses and contact details. You do not need to include your marital status or whether you have children

Research interests: This is optional, but you could include a couple of lines here to provide context to your application.

Academic career: This should include dates and locations of fellowships, postdoc positions, PhD lab, university (with degree status, you should include any transcript from your university as an appendix to your CV), senior school with final year subjects and grades. The most recent should come first.

Prizes: If nothing recent, include any final-year prizes from your secondary school.

Grants: Including grants that you have won for research (even grants for consumables), attending conferences, summer-projects and travel all add lustre to you CV. They show that you have had the energy to have applied for them and that other people have thought that you were worth supporting.

Research Experience: Such is the competition to get into good labs today that it is hard to be taken on for a studentship without research experience. Just about the only argument that will get you shortlisted with only an honours project under your belt is that you have done unexpectedly well in your project and degree exams and have also become particularly interested in some topic; as a result, you are now considering a research career. And your referees should back this up. If you want to boost your research experience, try to get taken on in a lab as an assistant (paid or unpaid) for at least a short period. Supervisors tend to distrust applicants who have not shown evidence of prior research commitment.

Working visits to other labs: These show that you can collaborate, are outgoing and have links outside your immediate lab.

Research skills: These are not mandatory for a PhD application but are for a postdoc position as PIs are keen to know what technical abilities you can bring to their lab, particularly those that their labs might want.

Talks and posters: You should go out of your way to produce posters of meetings as their entry on your CV shows that you have done something worth displaying.

Journal involvement: Include any paper-reviewing that you have done as it implies that other people have heard of you and that you are involved in the wider scientific community.

Responsibilities: Evidence here matters because it shows that you can take on leadership roles. As a graduate student or even as an undergraduate, you can organise a group at which you can invite speakers and give one another practice talks. A major concern of potential supervisors and PIs is that you might become a liability who cannot show initiative and will have to be helped to an unreasonable extent - you need to block that concern.

Teaching experience: This shows that you have experience of standing up in front of a class – a necessary skill for a budding scientist!

Public engagement: This covers anything you have done to bring science to the wider world, such as talking to schools and posting scientific material on a website.

Work experience not in research: This is more important for a PhD than a postdoc applicant, although, if too many jobs are not related to science, you may be asked why.

Other interests: These add colour and help give a rounded picture of who you are.

How to Become a Scientist

Referees: These are less important than you might suppose as most referee comment are polite. Experienced readers of CVs have learnt to look for what is not said rather than what is. Comments that carry weight include

> You have made a difference in a research lab.
>
> You are very clever, hard-working and committed.
>
> You rapidly got on top of some project.
>
> You completed difficult jobs on time.

Make it easy for them to write that reference! It is an added bonus if the recipient knows the referee, either personally or by reputation. Always ask people in advance if they would be prepared to act as your referee **and** support your application. First, they will be offended if you don't and this won't help! Second, it gives them the opportunity to decline. Reviewers tend to be honest and would rather not write a bad review[11].

Once your CV has been drafted and looks good, it is sensible to show it to someone senior and ask how it could be improved in content and/or layout.

Finally, although it is not part of your formal CV, you should assume that anyone thinking of taking you on in their lab will take a quick look at your Facebook page and other social media profiles. ***Hint****: If you have anything online that you would rather professional people didn't see, take it down, at least over the application period.*

CHAPTER 25: SENDING EMAILS

If you are still an undergraduate, most of your emails will, up to now, have been informal. Once you want a studentship or need to communicate with someone senior in academe or any other organisation, you have to get to grips with a different reality. Your emails are no longer just for chatting or making arrangements, but are written because you want something from a recipient whom you may not know and who may be in a position of responsibility; essentially, they are business letters. You have to know how to write in a more formal way if you are to be treated seriously.

It is important to realise that all written communication, even emails, send a subliminal message to a reader who has never met you or knows anything about you. Is the tone polite? Is the language appropriate? Are the spelling and the grammar correct? Is the email neatly laid out? If the answer to any of these questions is no, then the recipient will immediately get an image of you that you may not want to give. The reader will form this impression before they actually read the detail of what you write. ***Hint***: *If the email looks good, they will be reasonably disposed mood towards you. If it doesn't, they won't.*

The key to all written communications, indeed all types of communication from phone calls to lectures, is for you to put yourself in the place of the recipient and ask yourself if, when I look at the email or whatever, does it give a good impression of me. Only then should you reread the text and judge if it says what you want it to say and whether you make clear to the recipient exactly what response you want, be it a reference, an invitation to visit or some information.

If that email is important (e.g. you want them to see you with a view to taking you on as a graduate student), it might be sensible to draft the email as a WORD document. This not only avoids the risk of sending the email by accident before it has been polished (something I have done only too often), but allows you to sleep on the text, usually a good thing to do, and even to show it to other people. This is particularly appropriate if the request matters and you have little experience of writing formal letters. In this case it can helps to show the text to a current member of your academic staff and ask if the message reads well and whether you have left out anything significant.

Writing emails is just one of the ways in which you have to develop a public persona. In the professional world of science, very few people will know you as you are. How they appraise you depends entirely on how you communicate with them, through email, through publications, through talks and lectures and, in due course, through your administrative skills. Knowing how to handle all this well is part of becoming a professional.

CHAPTER 26: READING PAPERS AND LISTENING TO TALKS

You will spend a lot of time reading papers and listening to talks and this can easily become a passive habit to the extent that information goes in through one ear or eye and goes out of the other. It is therefore sensible to keep computer files and endnote references on everything that you read and to make a note of the goods and bads of every paper. A helpful frame of mind when reading and listening is temporary schizophrenia: as well as noting its subject matter, identify the reasons why this paper/talk is good, and then list the reasons why this paper/talk is bad.

The ability to listen and to read critically is a key skill that all scientists need to acquire as early as possible. One thing that you should always have in the back of your mind as you listen and read is whether the talk or paper suggests an experiment that you might do, a technique that you should be able to use or an idea that you might follow up. You also need to be thinking about where your career is going next, in terms of both topics and labs. For this reason, it is important to read more widely than is strictly necessary and to go to talks by good scientists, even if they are some way from your immediate area of research.

On a personal note, the direction of my career has been dramatically shifted three times: my choice of a biophysical PhD was determined by a talk by Max Perutz (the father of modern biology) when I was a physics undergraduate. My subsequent shift to developmental biology followed a talk by Lewis Wolpert at which he showed time-lapse movies of sea urchin morphogenesis – I was bowled over! Later, a complete change of research direction was initiated by a meeting that I went to because it sounded interesting, and it was!

Such active reading and listening becomes important when you have, as I hope you frequently will, to present papers and report on conference talks at Journal Clubs. To bring papers to life, you need to do more than just summarise them. It is important to add a personal view. For example: *This long paper discussed ......, however the key experiment was* ...... and you can then go on to give the problem, the reason why it mattered,

How to Become a Scientist

and the implications. You can end up by discussing the wider context and any aspects of the work that were inadequately treated (e.g. *I was however surprised that the authors didn't do the next obvious experiment...*).

At Journal Clubs, you may also have to report on talks given at meetings. As conference talks can be boring, your first task is to keep the audience awake. As it is hard to make a dull talk interesting, you need to focus on the good ones! As an example of what works at an informal Journal Club, try "*At such-and-such a meeting, I listened to 10 talks and only two kept me awake. These were ...*". If you know in advance that you are going to have to summarise such talks for your journal club, you can use your mobile phone at the meeting to take snaps of interesting slides and then polish them in Photoshop before reshowing them. This will add real heft to your presentation.

If your department doesn't run a journal club at which postgrads can contribute, you should start your own (and claim the credit on your CV). The ideal club has about a dozen people from different labs and will meet weekly. Sessions should alternate between a couple of paper presentations and a couple of work talks with everyone "performing" in turn. Having this will give you a forum at which you can learn to speak confidently in public to people who are not close to your work, where your future external talks can become polished and where hard questions can be asked in a non-confrontational way to give you experience of thinking on your feet. It can also give you a forum for getting to know other students and postdocs and talking to them informally about work.

There are always good reasons not to go to a Journal Club where you are not speaking, so there need to be non-academic incentives that make it worthwhile for people to attend. The two best hooks are to hold the club at a time when people are unlikely to have something better to do (e.g. lunchtime) and to provide decent coffee and good quality nibbles. If you are organising such a club, ask the Head of the Department or the Chair of the Postgraduate Studies Committee or anyone else who may have some spare money for small amounts to fund this important educational forum for postgraduate students. With luck, you may also find a senior academic who will be happy to sit in and add their perspective to whatever is going on.

CHAPTER 27: POSTERS

set as a reading

All postgraduate and postdocs have to produce posters and it is one of the best ways of advertising your talents. If you have spent many hours walking round poster sessions looking for something that you actually want to read, you will know how hard it is to produce a poster that will interest more than the very few people who care about the details of its topic.

The first task of a poster is to catch the eye of attendees wandering past and this is done partly by the title (large print) and partly by its general appearance – the poster as a whole looks good. Once a passer-by approaches the poster because of the title, they will then look at three things:

1: The font size to check that the text is readable.
2: The introduction to see if they can follow it easily and hence if they want to know more about the topic.

3: The logical structure to see if they can follow the scientific argument easily.

If your poster fails any of these tests, they will rapidly move on to something more enjoyable.

If, however, the poster looks good, is easy to read and communicates what you want to say in a way that is straightforward to follow, the benefits are considerable. First, you may win a prize (something for your CV) and second, you will find yourself discussing detail with many more people than you might expect, and this can lead to suggestions for future work and making new contacts. Even better, one of them may suggest that you visit their lab and give a talk, and this could even lead to a job offer.

Poster content

The question of whether the poster should include only your work or whether it should also reflect the work of several people is your choice. If you are showing only your work, then yours is the only name at the top of .the poster and members of the lab who helped are included in an acknowledgement panel. Doing this will give you a sense of personal pride, but it may not be politically sensible as you can gain brownie points by being recognised as part of a well-known lab. If most of the work is yours, put your name first, then come your collaborators with your supervisor or PI last – this is the normal position of the lab head. As to the font style, have just your name in bold and put everyone else in standard font. This will allow people to know who you are when you speak to them and help them to remember your name. Try to keep the list of authors fairly small so that the credit is not diluted too much; minor collaborators can be thanked in an acknowledgement panel.

It has to be said that planning a poster is difficult because you will usually have far too much material that you want to display – you are proud of all the work that you have done! If you feel that you want to and that there is space, you can always include a context panel saying that this work is part of a bigger project and detail the other components. Such detail may however best be kept for conversations with viewers.

The key first step in producing a good and clear scientific poster is to decide the single key question/hypothesis/technique that you want to ask/test/explain. Given the size of the poster and the limited attention span of viewers, this is the most that you can hope to communicate. This decision enables you to produce a title and an introduction. Only then can you move on to the associated text, graphs and pictures, making sure that you exclude anything that seems to be of secondary importance.

Designing a poster is also hard as you have to balance style and content so that the poster contains everything that you want to include, but is still easy to read, and at a distance of a least a metre. It also needs to be visually and scientifically attractive to the casual passer-by who might be two metres away. This is impossible if there is too much material in the poster because the point size of the text and the images will then have to be unreasonably small.

There are many meeting posters on the web in your subject. While you are still at the thinking stage, look at them and decide on a style that would, you think, not only suit your work but catch the eye of passers-by. If you don't get people to look at your poster, the whole exercise will have been a waste of time.

It is also important to ensure that the poster is self-contained so that it doesn't need you to explain it. You may want to spend a few minutes away from your poster and you don't want people miss the point of your work. If however you feel that you will need to be away from your poster at some point during the session, have a note ready that you can pin to it giving the time at which you will be back – just in case someone wants to talk to you. Some key points about posters are given in Table 27.1.

Table 27.1. In well laid-out posters .....

1: Title (60-72 point) and introduction are clear at a distance of two metres.
2: The poster as a whole looks good and is easy to navigate a metre away.
3: Headings are simple and introductions (~100-words)

are readable at 2m.

4: Aims are clear (question asked, hypothesis tested etc).

5: Results are clear, with each panel making a single point using minimal text.

6: Key methods only are included.

7: Text panels (20-24 point headings, 16-18 point text) are clear and short.

8: In graphs: only key data with good controls with error bars are included.

9: Pictures make a single point (using arrows if needed).

10: Conclusions refer back to aims.

11: There are small panels for acknowledgement, and for other and/or further work.

12: The colours add to the design and are not a visual distraction.

13: The poster is an advertisement that should look good because it has:

    A very clear organisation making it easy to navigate.
    A clean layout.
    A neat and pleasing sans-serif font.

Poster text

The key panels in a poster are the title banner and the introduction (better than a summary or abstract), both of which may be printed in the meeting handbook. There will also be panels for aims, methods, results, conclusions and acknowledgements. There may also be panels for references, context and future work. It is a lot to include in a single poster 841x1181 mm (A0, Europe) or either 914x 1219 mm or 864 x 1118 mm (USA).

Title

The title needs to be short (ideally a single line) and very focused so that any passer-by gets the point at a glance. The title banner will also include the authors and the lab details. If there is more than one address, consider having superscript numbers for each name and putting the numbered addresses in a smallish font in a panel at the bottom of the poster. There, you can put your contact email, important if anyone wants to follow up the poster.

Introduction

This has to explain the background to the work, the approach and the reasons why people should be interested, all in 100-150 words (no panel should be longer than this or you risk losing the reader). The intention is to intrigue the reader, even one only vaguely interested, and suck them into your narrative. This is the hardest text to write.

Aims

This key sentence has to be along the lines of: *The aim of the work is to*

   a: test the hypothesis that .... using ....
   b: answer the question of whether .... using ....
   c: produce a technique that .... using ....

d: develop a theory that ….. based on …….

The rest of the poster ties directly back to this aim. If there is a good reason, you can have more than one aim but it is usually better to group them under a single key aim which depends on answering two or three questions, Be modest in your aims; there is only so much that you can include in one poster.

Methods

This panel should not include minor technical details, but should focus on the system, the experimental manipulations and the assays. Only include further technical details if they are important.

Results

You will normally have too many results to show them all, and you should remember that the fewer you include the larger the text can be and hence the easier they will be to understand. The results should give only the key data (with controls and statistics) that are needed to meet the aims set out earlier. It is important that the viewer understands the flow and implications of the results without having to work too hard.

Conclusions

These should start with the direct implications of the result and then show that the aim has been achieved. You should also mention any other important observations and the general implications of the conclusions

Other panels

These may include **context** (see above), **future work** and **references**, but should be as terse as possible – single-line bullet points are always visually effective. You should always include an **acknowledgement** panel thanking people for their help. They will appreciate it when they see the poster, but you should mention to them in advance that they will be thanked.

Poster design
Organisation

Once you have the basic structure of the poster and a rough draft of what text will be in each panel, sketch out how you think that the poster will be structured so that it has a clear logical and visual progression.

Final text

Once the layout is clear, you can write the detailed text for each panel. Once you are happy with this, start being critical. Examine every sentence and cut every superfluous word. The fewer words there are, the larger can be the font size, the clearer will be the text and the easier the poster will be to read.

Text presentation

You need to choose a font that is easy to read. I like Calibri as it is an elegant san-serif font that looks good in both normal and bold, but other fonts may work. I would however avoid serifed fonts such as Times New Roman and Palatino: although serifs work well for small font sizes, bigger ones tend to look fussy and old-fashioned.

You will need a banner across the top of the poster that will include the title, authors and addresses. The **title** needs to be large enough that it can be read from across a room. 60 point is the minimum size, but 72 point (2.5 cm) is probably better provided that the title is short enough to occupy just a single line. The author list can be smaller (e.g. 48 point) while 36 point should be adequate for the address(es).

The test for the font size for the text panels is that they are easy to read at a distance of a metre. For my eyes, 16 point is just acceptable, 18 point is easy to read, and 20 point may be a little large for a body of text, while a text 4 points larger (normal, italic, italic/bold or bold, as appropriate) works well for headings. If you really do need a lot of text, you may have to go a little smaller, but try not to. The only text that can be as small as 14 point is that in captions for graphs and images: the reader who wants this information is normally close to the poster.

Delineating text in a coloured rectangular box with rounded corners always looks good but do ensure that the reading order of the boxes is obvious – if necessary, you can use arrows to show the route that the eye should follow.

Graphs

If you put too much material in a graph, you risk losing the reader. Your graphs should thus include baseline or control data and only enough extra material to make the necessary points. If there are just one or two points in a lot of data to which you want to draw the reader's eye, then put them in a second and bright colour. It should not be necessary to say that you must include control data and error bars, if appropriate – their absence makes readers suspicious and you look amateur. Don't forget to label both axes clearly: the aim is that the reader gets the point very quickly without having any concerns.

Images

Try to include images: they not only make a poster look attractive, particularly if they are coloured, but they also break up dull-looking text. If you don't have any, find something that is appropriate and eye-catching to include (e.g. an explanatory cartoon). If there is detail associated with specific colours, include a small table of explanation in an unimportant part of the image - this works better than including the explanation in the underlying or adjacent caption. If the image is a micrograph, you must include a size bar (this is better than a magnification) together with a control picture (never forget the old joke about how one can tell a scientist from anyone else: when you ask them how they are, they reply "compared to what?"). Captions should be short and emphasise the point that you want to make, just in case the viewer is not smart enough to work it out for themselves. Gels are visually dull so only include sufficient to make key points. What matters in all images is not that the viewer loves the picture (that is an added bonus), but that they get the point instantly. If that point is not obvious, add a few arrows to draw in the viewer's eye and explain in the caption what the arrows indicate.

Poster presentation

Once all the pieces are assembled separately, you are ready to fit them onto the PowerPoint slide that you will take to the printer, and this too is not easy. The ideal poster doesn't look crowded, but also doesn't have too much white space (this implies you don't have much to say). First ensure that your graphs, tables and images are a good size so that they can be "read" easily. Then insert the text boxes and see how the draft poster looks – it will probably be a mess. There is then an iterative process of cropping images and up- or down-sizing graphs so that they have the same width and look neat when they are aligned vertically. You will then play with font sizes so that the resulting panels, again of a standard width, look right. At this point, in a perfect world you have a good draft of your poster. In the real world, however, you will probably have to go back to your text and sharpen and shorten it a bit. Normally, the shorter the better.

Only now can you start to think about colours. Do you want white panels on a dark or light background? Do you want dark text panels with light text and a light surround? There is no correct answer to what works. You can do what you like, subject to the constraint that it has to look good and be easy to read. The design has to support your work and not distract from it.

Finally, show your draft poster to friends and colleagues, listen to their responses and act on them. We are always too close to our own work and the poster is not meant to impress us.

As to printing, most are printed on glossy paper and have to be carried around in long plastic cylinders. These can be cumbersome and expensive on planes as they may have to go in the hold. ***Hint**: Some companies will now print posters on cloth which can be folded and easily fitted into a standard bag.*

When the poster is finally complete, you may think that it doesn't do justice to everything that you have achieved, and I hope that it doesn't! This is why you might want to include the context panel. Alternatively, you can prepare some discussion points that you can *naturally* bring up is the course of conversation with interested viewers. But don't worry too much about being a bit minimal; it is far better that you say a little less than you would like but say it very clearly than that you say too much. In this case, you risk the passer-by either not being bothered to engage with your work or giving up because there is more in the poster than they can properly grasp on a quick read.

CHAPTER 28: GIVING TALKS

You will have sat through a great many talks and lectures. Most are long forgotten, and few are remembered with any pleasure. What you probably haven't done is work out why some were good, some were annoying, some left your mind free to do something useful, and some just sent you to sleep.

All talks[12] that are worth listening to start off by capturing your attention and then keeping it to the end. All talks that are worth remembering include a simple message, one that stays in the mind either because it adds something to your immediate interests, or because it carries some sort of a link to your wider interests, such as a stunning image, a completely unexpected fact or a counterintuitive conclusion.

This might suggest to you that the purpose of a talk is to give interesting information as clearly as possible. This however is only half of the story. Whenever you speak in public, you are advertising yourself and your ability, and it is a mistake not to realise this. If you are applying for a position, your talk has to be competitive. Most people being interviewed for a studentship or postdoc are reasonably clever, so you need to show more than this to convince people on the other side of the table that you have the makings of a good research scientist.

Some clues as to what impresses audiences are given below. Most student and postdoc talks are competent enough, but you need to aim higher.

Planning a talk

The first step in planning all talks is getting a clear understanding of the message(s) that you will want the audience to take away; the next is to write down a set of bullet points of the key new pieces of information that you will want to present. This has to be done in the context of how long you will talk for and an understanding of how much material you can include. Most talks given in public by younger scientists (e.g. interviews and meetings) are for ten or even five minutes and this is only enough time for a single topic, so you have to plan to be extremely efficient in the way that you present the "story". Table 28.1 gives you some idea as to what works for particular time slots, both for you as speaker and for your audience. If you don't include enough, you will bore them. If you try to present too much material in too short a time, you will lose them for two reasons.

First, you may make it hard for the listeners to keep track of you research arguments. It can sound as if you are trying to impress with how much work you have done rather than establish that the conclusions that you will reach are well-based. Second, you can overestimate the detailed knowledge of their listeners and forget that you (should) know more about your research topic than anyone else in the room. Aim your talk (unless it is to your own lab) at the level of an educated scientist in your field rather than at the specialist in your subject. If you do not spend time explaining what you have been doing and why, the audience as a whole may never really get the point of your talk. If the talk was part of an interview, you will not realise how much damage these mistakes have done until you get a completely unexpected rejection letter.

Table 28.1: The amount of material that can be put in a talk

5m talk - 1 small topic
Question and its importance, key data, techniques, answer,
10m talk - 1 small topic that should be complete
20m talk - 1 topic in depth or 2 small topics
If the latter, more time is needed for introduction & conclusion

> **45m talk** - a rich story that covers several topics
> Set out the structure in advance
> The main problems are
> Keeping the audience awake
> Keeping the audience on track and interested
> **Note:** Always keep within the allotted time
> No one will complain if finish a little early
> Talk for longer and you will irritate your audience

Time spent in planning a talk is never wasted and it helps to know how much time you should spend on each of its components. In a 10 (5) minute talk, you will probably need 3 (1) minutes for the *introduction* and 1 (0.5) for the *question/hypothesis* that you want to answer/test. You will probably only need 1 (0.5) minute for *core methods and assays*, but 3 (2) minutes for the *key experiments and results*, while the *answer/test and its implications* will take another minute. This adds up to 9 (4.5) minutes - the extra minute (30 seconds) will disappear as talking always takes a little longer than you expect when you have an audience.

The key to all good talks is to have a clear narrative structure that carries the audience, that leaves a clear message, and that fits neatly into your time slot. The simplest narrative structure is to ask a question and answer it or to put forward a hypothesis and test it. The audience should feel *I got the question - I now want the answer* and will be with you all the way. If you feel that you are telling a story with a punch line at the end, you will have a natural format that will carry the audience and make it easy for you to sound convincing. This structure should be good enough to handle all the talks that you will give in your next few years[13].

Note, however, that, although a single topic works well for a ten-minute talk, it would be unlikely to have enough heft to carry you through 30 minutes. For longer talks, you will need more material and a richer structure. This carries the added difficulty of organising transitions and making sure that everything links together. ***Hint***: *A useful trick here is to introduce the topic sequence early and remind people where you are by reshowing the slide with where you are now in black and the other topics in grey.*

Such a narrative has an added advantage: if you start off with a clear aim such as a question and use this to build up your argument, you can have the audience on tenterhooks waiting to see what happened, and almost willing you on to end up with a clear answer. The audience will have been given something that they can remember. If this is a talk for a competitive position, then you will be someone whom the panel can include in the few applicants that they can easily recall at the end of a long day when they meet to make a decision.

There is one other important point that you should remember when thinking about your talk and that is establishing that the focus is **you** and not your lab. Scientists have a tendency to say "We" when they actually mean "I", and this tends to mean that the audience is never sure what exactly you have done and what was the responsibility of other people in the lab. A good working rule is to say "I" when you did it and "we" or a person's name when someone else did a piece of work.

Hint: Claim the credit for what you have done and don't be overly modest.

Choosing the topic

If you have completed several projects and have a choice, choose the one that will give the clearest narrative and that is most likely to impress your audience or an interview panel.[14] If you do have several topics, you might mention them in an early slide and then give the reason why you have chosen to talk about a particular one today.

A problem that can occasionally confront undergraduates is that they have to give a PhD application talk before they have made any progress in their honours project and they don't have an alternate piece of work to present. The solution here is to say that you don't yet have results but that you would like to explain why you chose the honours project, why it matters, what you are going to do, what results you expect and what will be their significance. I have seen this strategy used, and such was the brilliance of the presentation that the panel was blown away. The chair had only one comment *Are we good enough?*

The title

This is a hook to get the interest of the audience; it should not include the answer and should be short. Thus, *The role of Msx1 in digit formation* is better than *Msx1 modulates digit formation*: the latter gives too much away too early and you will risk losing the audience before the how-it-does-it punch-line.

Written abstracts

The purpose of an abstract is not to tell the whole story – doing this gives any potential audience member a good reason *not* to go to your talk. You should view the abstract as an advertisement that makes that audience member want to come to your talk. It should therefore focus on the project, why it is interesting and how you have approached it. It should also be as short as possible and so easy to read.

The one exception to this rule is when the talk is to be given at a meeting whose abstracts are to be published (and you will then have a minor publication to add to your CV). In this case, you should choose a title which includes the punch line and an abstract that really does give a summary of your research work.

Introduction

You need to spend longer introducing your topic than you would think, because you need to explain your project and its context, why it matters, what are the problems and what exactly is the question/hypothesis/theory/technique you wanted to answer/test/expand/develop. If you do not spend enough time on the introduction, you risk losing those members of the audience (most?) who are not familiar with your area.

Material and methods

Unless the talk focuses on a new technique, this should be short and focus on the system and any key techniques and assays that might not be well known. This part may well include at least one slide that indicates the baseline data that you will be using next. Doing this has the advantage that your audience will have an easy, visual introduction to your system.

Results

It is important that you build up to your punchline in a very clear, step-by-step way making sure that you include all controls and statistics. The logic when you describe your experiments needs to be crystal clear so that people who know little about your topic can follow you. This is where your use of *PowerPoint* or *Keynote* is particularly important: it is easy to include so much data and so many images that your audience don't get your points instantly and have to focus so carefully on the screen that they miss what you are saying.

Words and slides have to mesh so that a glance at the screen is all that the audience should generally need. It is thus very important that the font is clear and the point size is large enough to be easily read. In practice, this is probably 16-18point. It is much better to have less material on a slide and make it clear, than to crowd your slides in the hope that people will be impressed with all the work that you have done - this never works!

One useful way of making material clear in a graph is to first include baseline data, then discuss what you did and only then add on top and perhaps in a new colour the key experimental data. Similarly, images, which can be hard to process quickly, need to be explained, so choose examples that are easy to interpret. Highlight novel experimental features with bright colours and/or arrows and always include scale bars if needed.

If your talk is a piece of theory, think of ways in which screens of equations can be made to look interesting. If your theory has made predictions that you have tested, you are unlikely to be able to cover everything in 10 minutes. In this case, it is probably best to skate over the steps of the theory[15] and concentrate on the predictions.

You cannot afford to show complicated slides that include data surplus to your line of argument. You can always have slides with advanced material in reserve ready to be projected later to help answer a sophisticated question (and doing so always impresses).

Finally, do not mention important results in public at too early a stage, such as before a paper is ready for submission or when your results may have patent or other commercial implications. This carries the risk that someone in the audience may try and publish before you or use your data commercially. This happened to me once and I still carry the scars! If you have any doubts as to how much you should say, discuss the work with your supervisor or PI before getting into the detail of planning your talk.

Discussion

The result section of the talk should end with the answer to the question that you raised in the discussion or to the hypothesis that you have tested. This section of the talk should be short and conclude with the implications of your work. The key point that you have to work on here is your last sentence. If you do not plan it in advance, you may embarrass yourself by having to say "*I think that I'll stop there*". The easiest way of ending the talk is to preface your last paragraph with "*Finally*" or "*To conclude*" so that the audience knows that you are about to end. Then work on that last sentence because it is likely to be remembered.

Acknowledgements

Be generous with thanking people both because it is the correct thing to do and because you never know who will be in the audience. An important question is whether the acknowledgements slide should be at the beginning or at the end of the talk. The latter is more usual, but the former has two advantages: first, it gives you an opportunity to impart information at the beginning as part of the thank you. Second, it enables your final slide to be a summary of what you have done which can be left up; this makes things easier for the audience to think about the questions they may want to ask.

Questions

In conference talks, people tend to ask straight questions about your data and its implications. In interview talks, things can be tougher and obvious topics include statistical analysis, other people's work and gaps in your data. In answering questions, you have to engage with questioners, even if you think that the question is stupid (here, be polite and take the question seriously). Your answers should be as brief as possible, and you need to know when and how to stop. Before responding, take a second to plan your answer. What helps more than anything else here are practice talks followed by hard questions - you need to learn how to think on your feet.

What should you do if you don't have an answer to a question? You should not say *I don't know*. What works better is to say that you don't have a direct answer but ....., and there are some helpful strategies for this.

Quickly think of an experiment that answers the question
It is on my to-do list!

Suggest a likely answer on the basis of your and other's work.

Point out that this is an interesting question in the wider context .....

i.e. change the subject!

The next level

What really impresses an audience? Most important is confidence; not the confidence that you display, but the confidence that audience has in you. It enables them to feel that they can relax knowing that they are about to hear a good talk.

Here, it helps if you appear relaxed but competent, and you achieve this by practicing your talk alone and in front of a home audience of your lab or other students and colleagues. Ask them for hard questions and feedback. Then revise your talk again. As an American friend once remarked to me *Where I come from, they say that you should never, ever give a talk for the first time*. Other pointers for putting an audience at ease are given in Table 28.2

Table 28.2. Rules for getting the audience on your side

1: Make certain that everyone can hear you.
Remember the politician's trick: speak to the person in the back row.
2: Don't speak too fast.
3: Ensure that the introduction is clear and comprehensible to the non-expert.

4: Give the aim of the talk early.
5: Ensure that each slide is easy to follow and just makes a single point.
Try to keep bullet points to a single line.
6: Have a summary slide of the key results and conclusions
7: Make sure that the audience can see you. Wearing black clothes when the lights are turned off can be counterproductive.

You can leave clues in the talk that you have done other experiments, so putting questions in the audience's mind that they can ask and you can answer.

Have a few extra slides available for after the end of the talk dscribing these further experiments. Having them creates a very good impression of serious preparation for your talk and of how much work you have done.

CHAPTER 29: INTERVIEWS

When you walk into an interview, you will probably notice that each member of the panel has a pile of paper in front of them and you may be concerned that your application may not be the most impressive. Don't worry! The reality of interviews is that your paperwork gets you an interview, but it is your performance in the interview that plays the major role in getting you the position.

The normal procedure for a studentship or postdoc interview is that you will be introduced to the members of the panel (don't bother to try to remember their names) and then be asked to give a short talk. You will normally have been warned of this in advance and should already have handed over your PowerPoint presentation, which should have been loaded onto the computer with your title slide already projected (***Hint***: *always have a back-up memory stick in case* *of emergency*). After the presentation, you will be questioned about the talk and the questioning will then broaden out, with the panel free to ask about anything. Finally, you will be asked if you have any questions. Once you have left the room, the panel will have a quick discussion that will probably result in their deciding whether you are someone to be considered in depth later, once all the applicants have been interviewed and decisions have to be made.

The talk and subsequent questioning should be straightforward if you have planned it carefully, practiced it a couple of times and been subjected to questioning from your friends and colleagues. However, you do need to ensure that the panel realises that it is your own work that you are discussing, not that of other members of the lab. You should therefore use "I" to emphasise your own work and "we" or a name for other people's contributions. If there is any doubt, they may ask you about your contribution to the design of project and how much of the actual work is yours.

Soon, the discussion will move on to wider matters, and it is a good idea have thought in advance about points that you will want to get across at this stage, if only to remind them of the strength of your CV. With luck, you will be able to mention these points naturally in your answer to apparently unrelated questions. Here are some of the questions for which you should have prepared answers.

What attracted you to the project for which you have applied? There are two sorts of answers to this question. First, you are interested in the research project because …. Second, you want to do this piece of work because it meshes with your long-term interests which are ….

Further questions that are designed to highlight your thinking about this project, such as *What are the key experiments you will do in the first year?*

What do you expect to be doing in five or ten years' time? Be honest, but academics tend to like people who want to stay in research and run their own lab.

What is the most interesting piece of research work you have done? And, if you are applying for a postdoctoral position, you really should be able to answer this one.

One problem you may still have to encounter is what to do about inappropriate questions based on your CV. These are usually addressed by men to women and examples are *Do you have children? If so, how will you look after them?* Or *You will have to move from wherever. How will your husband (they should of course say partner) cope?* One solution is to reply that it is not their business; this is correct but may not however be helpful. It is better to look at the chair with an expression that says "*Can he be serious?*" And give an answer such as "*I have already checked out childcare provision in the university"* or *"They will just have to move"*. A sparky response will earn brownie points from most academics.

Finally, when it comes to their asking if you have any queries, it is a bad idea to answer a bald *No,* as it looks as if you are not very interested in the position. A better response here is something along the lines of *No longer, I have checked out the lab and its work through speaking to Dr Whoever and my other questions were answered on the departmental website.* If you do have questions, you should have formulated them before the interview and an obvious example, of course, is *When will I hear whether I have got the position?*

Once you have left the room

You may feel that everything has gone well in an interview as there have been no arguments or difficult questions that you couldn't answer. This is not good evidence of a successful interview as there is a series of questions that the panel will have to think about whose answers come as much from the impression you have left as from your words. These include:

Has the candidate done their homework about the job and the department?

Will the candidate be a liability because they are incapable of taking responsibility?

Will the candidate bring anything new to the lab that will widen its abilities?

Is the candidate a robust and energetic person who can cope with lab life?

Will the candidate be a good colleague?

Is the candidate committed to the research project?

Is the candidate brilliant rather than just clever, with the potential to go far?

These are not questions that you can answer directly as the panel will not ask them directly. You can however intimate by your responses that the answers to some at least of these questions is *yes*.

A candidate can give a good impression by showing that they have done their homework, by talking clearly, by sounding enthusiastic, by having clear slides and by wearing appropriate clothes. For a science interview, this does not mean wearing a suit or looking formal, but you should look neat, tidy and respectable as this shows that you are paying some respect to the panel. ***Hint**: The basic rule is to dress for the position you want, not the one you have*. In practice, smart casual will usually do, but it is important that you feel confident in what you are wearing.

In short, prepare carefully for all aspect of the interview: the talk and its questioning, the wider questions, your questions, the unasked questions and how you are going make any important points, whether or not they arise during questioning.

CHAPTER 30: COLLABORATING AND NETWORKING

You should collaborate with other postgraduates and postdocs whenever possible. You should however remember that the key to a successful collaboration is that *you need one another's different technical abilities*. If you can both or all do the same things, you will inevitably argue, and the truth is that you actually don't need one another. ***Hint:*** *Early collaborations should be with just one, or occasionally two people to avoid the administrative load becoming excessive.*

Collaboration brings many benefits, whether you are in the same or in different labs. First, things will not only go faster, but you will both be able to achieve more together than you can on your own. Second, and if you are in different labs, you will broaden your network of friends and colleagues; even better, if you are in different countries, you will not only get the chance to travel but you should find it straightforward to get grants to pay for this (more for the CV). Third, you will learn a great deal.

Note that, whether you are a postgraduate or a postdoc, you need to let your supervisor or PI know what is going on before you start work. This is partly good manners towards the person whose future support you will need (you don't want a reference that suggests that you are a loose cannon), and partly because you may need to spend money, something that will require their signature. In addition, a good supervisor may be able to contribute insights.

There are two concerns that you should be aware of in collaborations. The first is lack of communication. This is unlikely if you are in the same or nearby labs, but it can happen if you are on different campuses or countries. The result can be that one of you thinks that they own more of the project than they should. The second comes when you are preparing papers for publication. It is easy for either one of you to think that you should be the first author. Here, the normal rule is that the main author should come first, but the price of coming first is that you have to do a lot of literary work. If there really is a balance of effort, then the easiest solution is to put the names in alphabetical order (standard in the computer sciences) with a footnote saying that the first two authors shared equally in the work – this allows you both to claim first-author status.

Networking

One of the compensations for the underpaid, insecure and overworked lives that young scientists live is that they can build an international network of friends who are smart and share common interests. The advantages are considerable: if you work at it, you can have sympathetic friends both locally and internationally. They are there now as a research resource and for having a good time with, but in the future as you all go your different ways, you will have people across the world with whom you can remake contact when you travel. With luck, they will put you up when you visit their town for, say, a conference. I cannot tell you how much more enjoyable it is to stay with friends you rarely see than it is to stay in a student dorm or a dull hotel. If you keep in touch, you will hear about jobs early, you will be able to collaborate with people you already know, and you will pick up general information and even gossip.

In, as it were, the real world, networks tend to be made up of working contacts rather than social ones. In academe, the distinction is blurred because postgraduates are very rarely in a competitive situation and their work is, by the standards on the non-academic world, relatively casual and communal. It is thus easy to meet people, to make friends and make your own network. Indeed, this is one of the real pleasures of academic life.

How to Become a Scientist

I would also urge every postgraduate to go out of their way to get to know people in disciplines other than their own – universities are almost made for this. You will be surprised how much you can learn, even from non-scientists! You will inevitably be overworked and busy, but do make a bit of time to indulge your non-lab interests in a social way – it may even keep you sane!

Networks decay if they are not maintained and this becomes harder as time passes and you see one another less. I recommend at the least sending New Year cards and emails, and making contact when something good or bad happens in the place where that friend lives. If you keep in contact with old friends regularly, if not frequently, it becomes much easier to get together when you visit their country or town.

CHAPTER 31: CHAIRING A SESSION AT A MEETING

One day, you will be at some small meeting and one of the organisers will come up to you and say: "Please chair the next session", and you will have no choice but to say yes. This short chapter gives you the basics of how to do this. The key thing is that the audience should feel that you are in control, but in an unobtrusive and unaggressive way. Once they get that feeling, they will expect things to go well and they almost certainly will.

The most important lesson in chairing that I have had came from a meeting that I attended when I had just started my first postdoc which was in a new area. I really was naïve and inexperienced, but I asked an unfriendly question of a well-known scientist and they avoided answering it. I was far too shy to follow up my question, but the chair did it for me by saying something like "That was a perfectly fair question and you haven't answered it. Do better". The chair was Francis Crick and I had the wonderful feeling that a Nobel Prize winner was on my side.

The lesson was that the chair is a referee between the speaker and the audience, ensuring that the speaker is given an opportunity to give their talk without interruption, but within their time slot, and that the audience can ask questions that will be properly answered[16]. In practice, being chair requires that you not only do this, but that you control all of the proceedings. You therefore have to do considerably more than just invite speakers to speak and to thank them afterwards. Here are some of the aspects of a meeting that are under your control as chair (see also Table 31.1).

Starting on time. Be in the hall early enough to check that all the talks are loaded onto the meeting computer or that there is a facility for people to plug their own laptop into the system. You may also need to remind people having coffee or tea that the next session will start in five minutes. You should also have checked that the first slide of the first talk is on the screen.

Introducing the session: Give the title of the session and perhaps a word about the general topic of the session. Then say that you will stand up two minutes before the scheduled end of each talk and you hope that everyone will keep to time. Then announce the name of the first speaker and give their title. The reality is that you will probably start a minute or two late.

Keeping to time. As you have warned, stand up two minutes before the talk is due to end. After one minute, say quietly "One more minute" to the speaker. A minute later, ask the speaker if they could bring their talk to a close. (Be a bit relaxed now: if you think that the speaker is coming to a natural end when you stand up, you may not need to say anything more.) Then thank the speaker and ask for questions. If the speaker doesn't appear to notice your warning, repeat it a minute later. If they don't finish within that minute, you have to be stern, even if they have more data slides that they clearly want to go through.

Questioning. If a lot of hands go up, you really have to take control of the proceedings. Choose the first three questioners and point saying we will take the first question from you, then you and then you. While questions are being asked and answered, keep looking round to see who catches your eye. Make visual contact and nod, then call on them once the previous question has been answered. Once you feel that you can only spare another minute for questions, you should say "I think that we have time for one last brief question" before you call on what will be the last questioner.

There are several problems that can arise during question time that and you need to know how to handle these if you are to remain in control, which you must.

There are no questions or only a single one. The obligation is then on you to ask a question to get things going. So, listen to the talk carefully and have a question that you can ask. It might be along the lines of the capability of the system or future directions or implications, but you should produce something. This is a matter of politeness and of kindness to inexperienced speakers.

A question is long, unfocused and is more of a comment than a question (***Hint***: *never ask or answer a question without working out how that question or answer will end*). This is tricky to handle but you can always ask the questioner to give the exact point of their question or to suggest that this is too detailed for now and perhaps the questioner and speaker can discuss this at coffee afterwards.

An answer goes on too long. Here, you stop the speaker by saying that the discussion must continue afterwards.

Do not feel embarrassed if you have to be a bit harsh. If the audience feels that the speaker or a questioner is not playing by the rules and you call them out, they will be on your side. Always, however, be polite (unless you are Francis Crick!).

The next speaker. Once you have thanked the speaker, the next speaker should be ready to come to the rostrum and you formally invite them up and give the title of their talk. Meanwhile, the person running the computer should have shut down the previous presentation and mounted the next one.

Finishing on time. This is difficult because there is always a one minute or so handover period between speakers that is not in the schedule, while most speakers want the full amount of time that has been allotted to them. In practice, you may be able to save the odd minute when a speaker gets just a few questions, but you shouldn't worry about ending up to five minutes late.

Ending the session. You should thank all the speakers, tell the speakers for the next session to load their talks onto the computer either now or by ten minutes before the next session starts, make any other announcements that the organiser has given you and invite the audience to be back in the hall promptly for the next session.

In an ideal session, everything goes right, you keep control of the timing and everyone enjoys the talks – you will have done an excellent job! The trouble is that you will get no credit for this - people will only remember you if things have gone wrong and this is not a memory that you will want people to have.

At the beginning of this chapter, I mentioned that you might be asked to be chair when you weren't expecting it and had no experience of the job. The best thing you can do to give you self-confidence when this happens is to already have had some practice by chairing sessions in journal clubs and the like when postgraduate students are presenting their work.

Table 31.1: Summary of chair responsibilities

1: Ensure that you speak loudly enough to be heard everywhere.
2: Ensure that the session starts and ends on time.
3: Ensure that each speaker starts and ends on time.
4: Ensure that the speaker can be heard.
You may have to check that the microphone works.
You may have to ask the speaker to talk more loudly.
5: Ensure that speakers are properly introduced and thanked.
6: Handle questioning.
7: Listen carefully to each talk and prepare a courtesy question that can be used if needed to start the questioning.
8: Tell speakers for the next session that their presentations should be loaded onto the meeting computer either immediately after this session or ten minutes before the next one starts.

CHAPTER 32: CHAIRING COMMITTEE MEETINGS

No one particularly enjoys committee meetings, but they are a necessary evil as groups of people sometimes have to decide things communally. The first job of the chair is to work out in advance what decisions will have to made and the order in which they should be decided. This will be done by setting these topics within the standard agenda that may include apologies, minutes and follow-ups from the last meeting, reports, any other business and the date of the next meeting. This agenda should be sent to the other committee members a few days before the meeting to allow a further version to be produced if there are any further items for inclusion that you have missed. (In a perfect world, of course, the committee will have a secretary who does this, but this rarely happens at meetings run by graduate students and postdocs.)

At the meeting, you need to be as efficient as possible in getting through non-contentious items to allow time for any difficult ones. Your aim is to be seen to be in control of the proceedings by moving business along efficiently. You should make sure that everyone has their say, but not for too long, and particularly ensure that no individual dominates the discussion. You must however do this courteously and in the lightest possible way: it is counterproductive if the chair is perceived as a dominating bully.

Meetings should be as short is possible, subject to decisions being properly made and the resulting action points, together with who is responsible for them, being decided. You should try to keep the length of a meeting to less than an hour as people's attention tends to flag after that. To this end, people sometime schedule meetings over a sandwich lunch or for 4 pm on a Friday afternoon.

The meeting

Agendas. Make sure that agendas have been circulated in advance and you have spare copies ready for those who have forgotten them. Check that the order of items is what you want.

Minutes. If minutes have to be taken, there should be someone deputed to make notes on their computer. If no one is prepared to act as the secretary, then you, as chair will have to do so, and a good place for this is your copy of the agenda. The key thing for minutes is that they include what was agreed; it is rarely practical to include individual comments, but this may be necessary if there are different opinions that need to be recorded. One thing that you must do is note any action that will result from the committee discussions and who will be responsible for it. The inclusion of these *action points* is an important part of the minutes and they should be in bold so that they can't be missed. Minutes should be written up and circulated as soon as possible.

New attendees. If people that you don't know are attending and there is a risk that you may forget their names, it is a good idea to have a sketch of the table and positions done in advance and you can mark the names and positions of people you don't know. Whenever there is someone new at an established committee meeting, it is customary to ask everyone to introduce themselves briefly.

Business items: get through these as rapidly as possible, subject to decisions being reached, even if this eventually requires a vote.

Any other business. Some chairs don't like *any other business* items as they can get out of control. Their solution is to ask at the beginning of the meeting if anyone will have any items that they will want to bring up at the end of the meeting. They then note the person and the item and decide the order in which they will call them. I have always been more casual at the end of the meeting and just gone around the table asking for AOB items, and have never had any problems.

Ending. At the end of the meeting, agree a date for the next meeting and thank everyone for attending.

Other points

Difficult problems. The hardest aspect of chairing is handling difficult issues. Here, it is important to speak to each committee member in advance on the details of the problem, the possible solutions and the views of each member, of so you know more about the problem than anyone else.

When the issue comes up, your job is to introduce it and then summarise the alternatives and perhaps suggest one way forward. You might then, for example, go around the table asking people for their comments. If the group is more than half a dozen or so, you might add that people should be brief. You should also ensure that they don't talk over one another. If there are a range of opinions, you should write down the various views, and who made them (it can be hard to remember who said what). When everyone has spoken, you should note points of agreement and move rapidly on the points of disagreement and suggest a compromise view if that seems best. In short, make it easy for people to agree, and preferably this will be along lines that you think are sensible.

If you feel that no agreement is possible, it may be better, if time allows, to postpone the decision until the next meeting. If this happens, you will need to do some serious politics. You could, for example, write and then circulate a position paper that considers the implications of the options in more detail than is possible in a meeting; alternatively, you could talk the matter over with power brokers (e.g. your head of department) and see what they will accept, or you could have private conversations with each member and see where compromise is possible. If you cannot agree a compromise, you can take a vote, but an agreed compromise is always better as it is less divisive.

Refreshments. One thing that puts a committee on your side is refreshments that are better than instant coffee and dry biscuits! Good coffee and good biscuits are well worth the small extra expense as they improve the general mood of people who may well wish to be anywhere else! If the meeting ends late and you have some spare money, I have never known any objection to a glass of wine or a beer being served afterwards, or even half way through if the meeting is going on into the early evening.

CHAPTER 33: WRITING GRANT APPLICATIONS

You will spend a disproportionately large proportion of your future as a scientist applying for grants and the sooner you start the better. Successful grant applications are adornments to your CV because they not only show that others have thought well of your work, but that you have shown the initiative to apply for them. In addition to the larger grants that are available for research projects, small grants are often available for postgraduate students to fund travel, equipment and consumables. Even as an undergraduate, you can apply for grants for summer projects.

The key thing that you have to keep in mind when you write any grant application is that the *strength of a grant application depends only on how it is read.* Grants that are hard to read, lack clear aims, justifications and benefits, and that fail to say precisely what you will do with the money are not viewed kindly at any level. The first aim of any grant is to convince the reader that they feel that this project is worth funding, the second is to reassure them that you are a suitable recipient.

Minor grants

This sort of grant is typically for travelling to a conference or for a small piece of equipment and the application is fairly straightforward to write. Once you have downloaded the application form, check submission dates. If the next submission date will be too late for the project you have in mind, discuss this with your supervisor. If the application is to a small internal fund, a phone call from them may lead to the rules being softened, or they may know an alternative source for the money.

As your application is for a small amount of money, what you write should be terse. It should, however, should include paragraphs or sections for at least:

The reason why you want the money.

The benefits that will accrue from it to you and perhaps to the field or the public.

Why you and your research merit the money.

A full list of costs and when the money will be spent.

The names of two referees who will vouch for you (and to whom you have shown a draft).

If there are any length restrictions for the application, make sure that you meet them. Once you have drafted the application, show it to your supervisor for comment and then polish it in the light of their criticisms. Meanwhile, check that your CV is up-to-date and looks good. Then read through everything again and polish it again; you should feel pleased with the result. Finally, ensure that you submit the application and CV before any official submission date.

Large research grants

These are intended to pay the full costs of any research project, and applications may have to cover wages, consumables, equipment, travel, publications costs and overheads (many universities add a 25-55% charge to grant applications in order to cover the full costs of running the lab). Full research grants extend from just enough to pay for a summer student project all the way up to the very large amounts of money needed to run a major lab for five years and cover the full costs of supporting a PI, postdocs, postgraduates, technicians and their consumables and equipment, together with their overheads.

Such applications can therefore be very expensive to fund and are consequently looked at more closely than small ones; research scientists consequently spend large amounts of time writing them. You are unlikely, as a postdoc, to be involved in much other than the research component of the application, but you do need to know about everything that goes in – it may not be so long before you yourself are going to be responsible for writing one.

What matters when you write such grant is that you feel that you have some hoary old academic looking over your shoulder as you type who will occasionally nod with approval, but will generally be saying "Do they expect me to follow that?" or "Call that a reason for spending money?" or "That control doesn't impress me!" If your prose and data are not convincing to experienced scientists, you will not get funded, irrespective of how senior you are.

Good grant applications have
    A strong introduction with:
        Clear aims.
        Clear justifications for those aims, based on the literature.
        Convincing preliminary work.
    An adequately detailed research programme
        A set of planned experiments showing how the initial aims will be met.
        Good baseline controls.
    Good supporting material
        General scientific reasons why the research is worth doing.
        Reasons why the public should be interested.
        A convincing explanation of all of the

costs.

Reasons why each of the listed personnel is required.

Visual appeal

They are clearly laid out and not cramped. They include:

Images that provide information and also look good.

Graphs whose significance is obvious.

Solid statistical analysis as appropriate.

They are well written with no spelling or grammatical mistakes.

Grant applications that meet these criteria automatically pass the first stage of reviewing: the referee glances at the document and immediately feels that the project looks good. You need to ensure that they keep this sense of goodwill as they read it carefully. If this happens, then the reviewer will know that the person who wrote it is clearly scientifically competent. They will consequently be able to judge the application purely on the quality of the science without any concerns about the applicant. Their report may also comment on the quality of the application.

Before you set out to produce this wonderful document, read through a successful grant application and talk to the person who wrote it. Get all the advice you can before you start to write, and show good drafts to colleagues for feedback before you submit it.

CHAPTER 34: OTHER TRANSFERABLE SKILLS

If you are in the sort of university that takes transferable skills seriously, you will see that their website offers a broad range of such skills and you should check out the list to see which of the courses you feel is worthwhile attending. For all of its hoped-for value, this book is certainly not the last word on the subject!

The most important of these skills is **language**. You will need to be confident in speaking the language of your lab and in writing the language of your future thesis (normally English). If either is not your first language and you still feel uncomfortable in it, make sure that the university to which you apply runs courses on speaking the local language and on strengthening written English - and take them. If English is not an easy language for you, take every opportunity that you can to strengthen your spoken and written English. Even native speakers of English should work at polishing their prose: an inability to produce clear, straightforward English prose sends a bad signal to anyone who has to read their writing.

There are two further skills that every young scientist should acquire: **statistics** and **programming**. Statistics deals with the key question of whether your apparently impressive results could have arisen by chance. All experimentalists should have a basic understanding of the subject, with the absolute minimum being a facility with the set of statistical tools offered by Excel, together with understanding of the circumstances under which each can be used. You need to be in command of these tools when you write up your PhD thesis as you will be expected to be able to explain what you have done and why.

You can, in principle, get through a PhD not being able to program, provided you are not a theoretician. However, the need to be able to set up websites and program interfaces, handle and manipulate large amounts of data, solve equations, produce cladograms and other graphical summaries, and analyse DNA is becoming ever more important, and an inability to be able handle the computational side of your area will hold you back. My advice would be to do a programming course as soon as possible and sensible languages to start with are Python and SQL, the language for querying relational databases. Part of your education as a postgraduate student is to ensure that you do a small project that uses these skills.

Having statistical and programming skills carries another advantage. In the future, when you are applying for postdocs, those labs whose computational and statistical skills are weak will see you as a desirable person to employ. Even if you leave research in the future, these computational skills will be useful in many other contexts and will always look good on your CV. They will look even better if you have a certificate confirming those skills.

Jonathan Bard

About the author

Jonathan Bard is Emeritus Professor of Developmental Biology and Bioinformatics at the University of Edinburgh. He did postdocs at Harvard University and at the MRC Human Genetics Unit in Edinburgh, where he then worked for more than twenty years, setting up its first postgraduate training programme. After he moved to the University of Edinburgh, he was a Principle Investigator for nine years on its Wellcome doctoral training programme, one of the earliest to be set up in the UK. He was then appointed Director of the Graduate School of Biomedical Sciences. Although his first degree was in physics, his research has mainly been in experimental and theoretical developmental biology, systems biology and, most recently, evolutionary biology.

After his retirement, he moved to Oxford where he is a member of the Postgraduate Committee in the Department of Anatomy, Genetics and Physiology at the University of Oxford and a graduate advisor at Balliol College.

---

[1] In the mid-1950s, Mossbauer, then a postdoc, noted that an expected peak of nuclear resonance wasn't there. He then worked through what was happening and was awarded the Nobel prize for physics in 1961.

[2] There is good online material about supervisors, and that on findaphd is particularly sensible.

[3] The most liberating thing that was ever said to me was made by a distant aunt who was a professor of bio-

chemistry. I was grumbling about how dull my area of graduate research was (the biophysics of collagen fibril assembly). She looked at me as if I was mad and simply said "You are not married to collagen". A year later, I was on my way to becoming a developmental biologist, and it was the best academic decision I ever made.

[4] At this stage your basic statistical analyses should have been completed, unless your thesis has produced vast amounts of data and its analysis is the point of the research.

[5] This chapter is not about papers for which you have made a secondary contribution. You will want that authorship, but you are not in control here. What should happen is that the senior author of the paper should contact you about what they want to include and ask you to draft some text and images/figures/tables. A little later, they will show you a draft so that you can check that you are happy about the description of your work and that your data is formatted properly. Even secondary authorship demands that you take responsibility for any of your work that is published.

[6] An asterisk is used to mark the name of the corresponding author who handles communications with the publisher and hence is the senior author who takes overall responsibility for the paper.

[7] Paul Dirac, one of the UK's greatest physicists, was asked how as a young man he was able to write his ground-breaking but long book on quantum mechanics so rapidly. He is said to have replied that he had been taught at school never to start a sentence until he had worked out how it would end, so he didn't have to correct his first draft!

[8] I have only had to do this once and the real reason for the very poor thesis was that the student's supervisor had died, and the department had not found another ap-

propriate one. We eventually found a good lab and a new supervisor in a nearby department prepared to take on that student. The thesis resubmitted a year later caused no concerns. But it was a lot of unwanted work for the examiners.

[9] Bringing a notebook to the oral is sensible in case you want to write something down or you feel that an answer would be strengthened by drawing a diagram. This will look better if your pen draws strong lines so that the diagram is easy to read. You may also want to bring some water as exams typically take at least two hours.

[10] You should never forget the words attributed to Sam Goldwyn, a legendary Hollywood film director: "a verbal contract isn't worth the paper it's written on!".

[11] The reviewer for a student applying for a prestigious PhD programme that I was part of wrote "This is not the sort of student you are looking for". This honest comment saved everyone a lot of bother, but the student really should have asked the reviewer in advance if they would be willing to act as a referee and support them.

[12] This chapter focuses on interview, seminar and conference talks. Journal club talks are considered in Chapter 26.

[13] There are, it should be said, no absolute rules here. I remember the head of my research unit giving an unprepared talk to a class of graduate students having picked up a random handful of slides from an earlier talk (this was in the 1990s). He apologised for his lack of preparation but, even though he broke every rule in the how-to-give-a-talk manual, he was brilliant: he wove a narrative around those apparently unconnected slides that made perfect sense and ended with a series of important points for the students to remember. I did however have to warn the students afterwards that his

immediate preparation may have been five minutes, but he had been giving talks for 30 years. Perhaps the lesson from this story is that giving talks gets easier, if and only if you learn from your experience.

[14] I recently heard a student give an apparently excellent talk on a clever piece of software that they had written to analyse an aspect of mouse behaviour. The panel was not impressed because the student had been working on a different project and immediately wondered why they had become distracted and what they had to hide about their real project.

[15] A useful comment for skating over theoretical detail comes from Turing (*Phil. Trans.* (1952) **237B**, 37-52) who wrote that: "It can be shown with some trouble but little difficulty that ....".

[16] I have never had the gall to be so rude to a speaker, but have on several occasions supported a questioner by asking the speaker to give additional detail to their answer.

Printed in Great Britain
by Amazon